CANS IN THE DRYER
(WHY CAN'T I JUST LEAVE?)

FROM TRAUMATIC BONDING TO FREEDOM

BY

ANNA POTTER

Xulon
ELITE

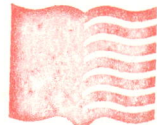

Cans In The Dryer (Why Can't I Just Leave?)
From Traumatic Bonding to Freedom
by Anna Potter

Printed in the United States of America.

ISBN 9781498446044

www.xulonpress.com

"The author of this volume is a woman I admire and respect for her candor, character and courage. She escaped the emotional prison of a controlling and frightening man, suffered the profound injury of complex post-traumatic stress, but recovered her dignity and never lost her compassion. Her story will inform and inspire."

-Frank Ochberg MD, psychiatrist and pioneer in trauma science, who served on the committee that defined PTSD.

"Cans in the Dryer is Anna's poignant story about how she overcame a situation millions of people find themselves in: a relationship filled with domestic violence. I was deeply touched by Anna's persistence and courage, even though she was frightened about her future and struggled with PTSD from childhood abuse, exacerbated by domestic violence. This book offers hope and validation. Those who feel stuck in abuse will learn about Anna, a woman who decided to fight for her freedom. Even though Anna was 'lost at sea' for many years, she rose, and reclaimed her life so that some of her dreams could come true."

-Joyce Boaz, Director, Gift From Within- PTSD Resources for Survivors and Caregivers www.giftfromwithin.org

"Only those who have experienced the pangs of a nonsensical, denigrating, dysfunctional marriage relationship can clearly express the sadness and grief it brings to the human spirit. Yet because so many find themselves in just such an unintended, unanticipated dilemma, THIS story needs to be told...to give hope to others. After much prayer and preponderance, Anna Potter has found the courage and the voice to tell her story. You may be just the one who needs to hear it."
-Dr. Wayne Flora, retired pastor of 34 years and adjunct professor, Lee University and the Pentecostal Theological Seminary.

"Cans in the Dryer (Why Can't I Just Leave?) clearly illustrates the oppressiveness of an abusive relationship and the complexity of leaving one. I hope it gives hope, strength and a guide to escape to those who are still trapped".
-Marla Handy, author of No Comfort Zone: Notes on Living with Post Traumatic Stress Disorder.

"Cans in the Dryer gives insight into the world of domestic abuse and the dynamics of escape. Anna Potter shows courage and strength as she delves into a subject in which the outside world is often afraid to tread. Through revealing both fears and insights, Cans in the Dryer illuminates the different aspects of abuse as well as the resources it takes to survive it."
-Amy Menna, Ph.D., LPC, contributor to Gift from Within.

Contents

Dedication

This book is dedicated to:

God, foremost. Thank you, Abba, for always being with me. (Psalms 27:10)

My husband, Jim, the most important person in my life, who made this possible and defines the term *soulmate*. I love you more than words can say.

Aunt Anna, the kind of mother I wish I'd had. You have been a comfort to me my whole life.

My confidante, Dr. Frances Buck, for honesty when it hurt, acceptance when I was goofy and her ongoing friendship. I truly appreciate and am thankful for you.

My therapist Rena Conley who gently taught me so much. You started me on the path to healing.

Joyce Boaz and *Frank Ochberg*, Director and Founder, http://www.giftfromwithin.org. You helped me understand how devastating trauma can be.

Dr. Jerry Flora, retired professor, Ashland Theological Seminary, who exemplifies the gentle, powerful love of God. Your friendship and correspondence have always lifted me up.

Jennifer Bull, a comfort in the midst of the storm. You and John are an inspiration.

Wayne and Lou Flora, faithful friends and prayer warriors. A thousand German Sweet Chocolate Pies could not repay you.

My awesome step-daughters for acceptance and the incredible gift of letting me be "Gammy", something I never thought I'd get to be.

All of my wonderful, supportive friends, past and present.

Charlie, my precious sidekick. You are the best birthday present I ever received.

Que Sera Buck, a very special therapy dog. You were greatly loved and are missed by many.

Que

Blaming the Victim

*W*omen in abusive and controlling relationships are often viewed negatively. Outsiders, family, professionals and law enforcement don't understand "why" the woman stays, and they begin to blame the woman for not changing what she could by leaving. There is even a direct quote by George DeBecker in his book, Gift of Fear: "Hit me once, shame on you. Hit me twice, shame on me." There are so many factors that affect women in abusive or controlling relationships which make it difficult to remove themselves:

One is their early history of growing up in abusive or neglectful homes, which forms how they perceive themselves, others, and what is normal.

Secondly, they learned early on that they weren't worthy, needed approval from others, and weren't good enough.

Thirdly, these women learned as children that everything that happened was their fault, and they caused their parent's anger and behavior. More damagingly, by assuming the blame or responsibility, it gave them the perception of being able to predict and control what they were experiencing. The abuse or neglect was bad enough, but we humans find the most distressing stress to be the sense we can't predict, avert, or have control over bad things happening. It is a bit of a paradox. The reality is that these children didn't cause the parent to act in any way, yet, they feel safer, more secure, if they think they did because then they could change the situation. Helplessness and unpredictability are the most devastating issues for people of any age.

Fourthly, there is ample evidence that people blame the victims rather than the true responsible person or circumstance because, by blaming the victim, then it can't happen to them.

By the time these women are adults, these patterns are established and thus are prohibitive to attributing accurately who is responsible and what their choices are. The most insidious aspect of any kind of abuse, no matter the age, is the undermining of a person's sense of reality and belief that their perceptions are valid. Blaming themselves causes them to distrust their perceptions, thoughts and feelings. How can one then see what is happening to them when they never learned to trust themselves that they were truly being victimized?

In adulthood, apart from these psychological issues, there are many societal, interpersonal, financial, and legal barriers. In some cases, their very lives are jeopardized. The very real fear of being endangered physically, harassed, stalked, bankrupted, etc. more by the abuser, after he's put out of control by the woman's leaving, should not be underestimated. Verbal abuse, control and unpredictable angry outbursts, over time, are "insidious and cumulative" to adult women. Even for women who didn't have as much trauma growing up, exposure over time with an abusive person begins to undermine self-confidence, self-worth, and sense of mastery.

Frances Marks Buck, Ph.D.
Clinical Psychologist

<u>Disclaimer</u>

I am not a counselor and this is not a self-help book. It is my story, depicting many years of trying to escape an abusive marriage. It is a journey that had to go backwards before I could go forwards. I have been completely transparent because I wish many years ago I'd had this story to read. I hope my brutal honesty will help others, in similar situations, show themselves compassion, and garner the courage to start leaving.

Names have been changed to protect privacy.

My favorite word in our language is "grace". When another shows me grace it's like finding a wonderful treasure in a barren wasteland. When I show someone else grace is when I feel closest to God. I hope readers will show grace, not judgement, for I am my own harshest judge.

I loved God and felt Him with me as a child, when He answered a silly, yet miraculous prayer; a simple act of grace that stayed with me through the years. I am proof that His grace really is sufficient and His strength is made perfect in weakness (2 Cor. 12:9). He never let me go. We serve and honor Him by helping others so I hope my story helps someone to begin that journey to a better life, sooner than I did.

Introduction

"You only ordered three packs of rice cakes?" My husband asks, unpacking a box.

"Yes," I reply.

"That's not nearly enough. We needed at least four, maybe five."

"I can pick some up at Winn Dixie if we run out. And I'll order more next month."

"Okay."

Suddenly I marvel at the fact that I'm having a normal, calm discussion with Joel. How life has changed! I still have moments when the past comes crashing in, an uninvited guest. But for the most part life is great.

This same scenario with my ex-husband, George, would have been much different. My *mistake* would have brought on a tempest, complete with red face, spittle flying, veins bulging, hostile cat-like eyes and words turned into missiles. My error would cause chaos in his life that demanded order, where everything had to go as planned, or else. I'd have been reminded how stupid I was, that rice cakes were more expensive at Winn-Dixie, that I was throwing away money and that I never listened to him. He'd be angry the rest of the day. "Why don't you just go out into the street and start handing our money out to strangers?" Sometimes I could hide my "mistakes", but even then I was scared out of my mind.

Still pondering my past, another instance came to mind:

I knelt in front of the dryer, looking over my shoulder, my heart racing, my breathing fast and shallow. I held my breath and listened. Was he coming? I watched the door leading to the kitchen and inched my hand forward. Would the doorknob turn before I got it inside, closed the door and rose to my feet?

In nanoseconds, I considered what would happen if it did: The door would open suddenly and he would look at me suspiciously. "Anna, what are you doing?" I would reply pitifully, "Nothing" or quickly make up a lie, "Checking to make sure the dryer is empty." But that excuse wouldn't work unless it was Friday because I was only allowed to do laundry on Fridays. "Okay, think Anna," I would say to myself. "I'm missing a sock and I was checking to see if it was in the dryer." No, that wouldn't work either. He'd rush over, jerk the door open and look himself, all the while berating me for losing a sock. Oh please God, and then he'd find it and then what could I say?

I placed it the dryer and quietly closed the door, my head pounding with adrenaline. I'd made it! Tears of relief blurred my vision. I made a mental note to remember to take it out the next time he left the house, or when he was in the shower; take it out and bury it deep in the trash can and then take the trash out because he would go through the trash sometimes. I felt dizzy with panic as I thought about what would happen if I forgot to take it out.

Weak with relief I sank to the floor. I was so tired of this. My mouth opened and I howled silently (yes you can howl quietly). I tried to keep the tears inside, but they seemed to hit my stomach like acid.

Suddenly the door opened. It was him! "What's wrong, Anna?" How could a question that is supposed to show concern sound like a gunshot of blame? And why did my name sound like a hateful thing when he spoke it? "I felt a burden for someone at work and I had to stop and pray for her," I lied. But at least he wouldn't look in the dryer and find it. Once again I'd lied to save myself.

I always had to think ahead. I had become a master at making up lies on the run. "What a talent to have," I often thought sadly. I was also a master at preparing for every possible worst-case scenario, a defense mechanism that had become a normal part of my life. Imagining the worst that could happen, I often had intrusive thoughts of tragedies and how I would deal with them. I call them "flash forwards". If I imagined the worst that could happen, then it wouldn't take me by surprise. It was difficult to enjoy fleeting moments of happiness when this underlying hypervigilance ruled my life.

"What's wrong with me?" I often asked myself. "Why can't I just leave?" Others who asked me that were not my allies. If they knew how badly I wanted out, they'd never have asked why I stayed. They would never have asked me if I liked being abused.

If I tell my story, they will understand. And maybe if I write this, it will all make more sense to me, too. Maybe I'll be able to forgive myself for the wasted years, if having lived them can help someone else. How did I get here? How do I get out? Was the answer in my past?

PART I

Little Victims...

On the porch of "the apartment" behind grandma's house

The first man I loved was daddy. Everything that happened to me in life would directly point back to him, even to the point of putting cans in the dryer.

Chapter 1

God's Country

*I*f you want to live close to heaven, travel Highway 26 through Asheville, North Carolina, into Tennessee. Continue past Elizabethton and Erwin, and stop in Johnson City. Find you a parcel on the side of a hill with a view of the distant mountains and build you a house in God's Country. I've watched family members leave only to return years later. The mountains get into one's blood and pulse there with every heartbeat. The pulse beats in the ears, calling one back to those hills, mountains, gaps, hollers and valleys. You can take the girl out of the mountains, but you can't take the mountains out of the girl. My grandparents and parents were born and raised there, their stories burned into my memory. Grandpa recited them on the porch swing, as we rocked gently back and forth to the comforting creak of the chain. And while I listened, those ever-present mountains stood in the distance like silent guardians.

House in Shady Valley where my dad lived in 1935

I loved life there, but daddy had to follow the jobs and the jobs took us away, down mountain roads bordered by rocky hillsides. The day we left I watched the rocks, looking up out of my car window, wondering if they might roll down on us as sometimes happened. Looking back, those boulders were like harbingers, reminding me of the tragedies that would roll down on us and carry us into the abyss.

The tragedies would start in Bensalem, Pennsylvania in 1963, but that wasn't our first move. We lived in many towns before I even started school. Memories are few before 1963, but the ones I do recall are the ones that did the most to form me. There had to be happy memories too, but they are trapped somewhere along the neuron highways in my mind.

Putting the time line of my life together through journals and photos has been dizzying. It was a necessary journey that I hoped would hold the pieces of the puzzle of the present. It was my last hope as I tried to escape an impossible existence, and it started once I admitted I was a victim of domestic abuse.

We moved at least fifteen times before I turned nine, daddy being a boilermaker and a union man. Moving so much doesn't contribute to stability. It doesn't have to be chaotic or traumatic, but a child is only as safe as he is loved and only as stable as his parents are wise.

May 1956, Tullahoma, Tennessee

My first move came when I was a year old and it was to Tullahoma, Tennessee. I'm standing in front of mom who is holding a friend's baby.

Tullahoma, Tennessee 1956

May – October, 1957, Bay City, Michigan

When I was three, we moved to Bay City, Michigan where, one day, mom put me out to play and forgot about me. I took off with the little boy next door, walking down the sidewalk pushing my baby stroller. Somehow we safely crossed streets and kept walking until the houses looked strange and we weren't sure how to get home again. We slowly crept on until a police cruiser pulled alongside, rescuing us. I remember how I felt when I realized we were lost, but I don't recall the other time that mom says I got lost. She wrote it in my baby book:

"In 1957 while living in Bay City, Michigan, she [Anna] went off with a little boy and got lost. She was gone so long we called the police. She also got lost when we were on one vacation trip in 1959 at the Hotel we stayed in in New Iberia, LA."

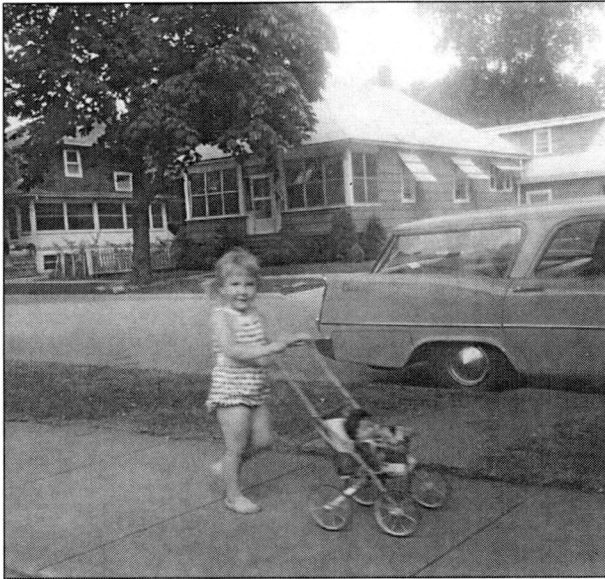

Safely back home in Bay City

January 1958, Chicago, Illinois

Another incident made me question daddy's character.

26

Daddy took me to the park on Lake Michigan today. I ran up to the railing and stared as far as I could, but I couldn't see the other side of the lake. It looked like the ocean! Spotting the biggest sliding board I'd ever seen, I ran over and started climbing the ladder. I was up so high. I could see for miles. I slid down over and over as daddy watched.

Another daddy and little girl came and she started sliding down, too. I liked her and we laughed together. One time she was in front of me. She wanted me to go first, but I told her to go. Then she said, "You go" and I said, "No, you go" until finally I said okay. I reached up and grabbed the bars to climb around her and for some reason, while leaning back to let me up, she let go. She fell. I kept watching and she landed on her tummy. Her daddy ran to her and lifted her up. Her face was mashed and bloody. I kept looking until I heard daddy calling to me. It sounded funny, like he was far away. "Slide down," he said but I couldn't move. He kept telling me to slide down and finally I did.

When I got down, I was looking over at my friend and her daddy was holding her and crying. Daddy grabbed my hand and tugged me hard. "Come on," he said. But I kept looking back as he pulled me towards our car. Finally he picked me up and almost ran to the car.

I was too scared to ask daddy, but I didn't understand why he wasn't helping the other daddy. Why would he just leave like we did something wrong? And was my friend okay? I really wanted my daddy to help my friend and her crying daddy.

27

Late January 1958, Waukegan, Illinois

Our next move was to Waukegan, Illinois. I was four and I got poison ivy so bad I was miserable. Kenny, my brother, said if it got in my eyes, I could go blind. Mom finally took me for a shot, after my whole body was covered in welts. The doctor told her not to wait so long the next time. That's all I remember about Waukegan. (*Ironically my second husband, Joel, was born and raised near where I lived in Waukegan. He probably attended school with my brother, Kenny.*)

May 1959, Clinton, Missouri

Next we moved to Clinton, Missouri. Mama took me to swim at City Park one day. It was fun and it was just mommy and me. I ran to the pool one time and fell on my butt and it hurt. But it was a good day.

The pool at City Park

Another day in Clinton mommy took me with her to the dentist's office:

Mommy and I went to the dentist today and his office was his apartment. We waited so long I had to pee. I told mommy and she said to hold it. After she saw the dentist, I really had to go bad and I begged her to let me pee before we went home. She acted like she didn't hear me and took me to the car. I asked her why she didn't let me pee. She said she didn't want to use the dentist's bathroom because it was his home. By the time we got home, I had to pee so bad I couldn't move. The bottom of my tummy hurt. Mommy parked in front of the house and got out. When she slammed her door it made my tummy burn. I thought she was coming to get me, but she walked in the house like she forgot me. It was hard to open my heavy car door, but I got out and limped slowly to the house. When I walked in I looked around for mommy on the way to the bathroom. I didn't see her, so I went and got on the potty. I had to sit there and push a long time before any pee would come. I was afraid I would have to go to the hospital for not being able to get my pee out. It took a long time to get all my pee out, but it still hurt down there. I never said anything to mommy, but somehow I knew she didn't act like a mommy should.

A little girl doesn't want to think her mommy is bad, nor does she want to believe that mommy doesn't love her. I didn't know the meaning of "neglect", but, looking back, her neglect caused physical suffering for me many times and almost proved fatal once. I had another brother who died of TB before I was born. I wonder if mama waited too long to get him help, too.

Mommy used to make my clothes and wrap my long hair in rags to make it cascade in long curls. My memory of her is filled with inconsistencies. Daddy told me later that she acted like I was a doll to dress up, but that he was the one who took care of me when I was sick. Unfortunately, he was gone a lot, leaving us at her mercy. I reckon our guardian angels worked overtime.

During the summer of 1959 we made a road trip through all the states. I have pictures of my brother, Kenny, my sister, Jean and I at all of the state welcome signs. I don't remember it, but the pictures show us smiling. Then we moved back to Bay City from February 1958 to November 1959.

December 1959, Johnson City, Tennessee

In 1959 we moved back to Johnson City, to the house behind grandma. Grandpa and daddy had built that house and called it "the apartment". Mom was not happy being so close to daddy's parents and Aunt Violet, who lived with them. Mom was intimidated by them and wanted daddy to take us with him on his jobs. She got depressed and sought the counsel of a nearby pastor after I started school. My grandparents used to glance at each other like they had a secret when they would talk about the pastor coming to see mommy.

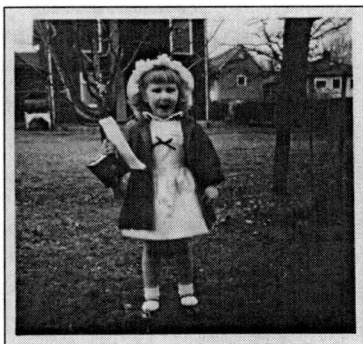

Grandma's house at 419 West Maple Street;
the apartment behind it

When I was four and a half I caught a sore throat while daddy was away, and it turned into strep. My fever got high, but mommy didn't take me to the doctor. Days went by and I became sicker. One night I went to pee and blood came out. Daddy happened to be back home that night and he rushed me to the hospital. I lost consciousness as he carried me in to Memorial Hospital where they found me near death. My blood pressure was so high I almost lost my hearing. The doctor told daddy if I survived I might still end up with Scarlet Fever and heart problems. The strep had turned into nephritis, an infection of the nephrons in my kidneys. Daddy had gotten me there just in time for the doctors to pour antibiotics into me.

Daddy sat up with me all night that first night. I'm not sure how many days I was in there, but I have the church bulletin asking for prayer for their daughter who was in critical condition. I remember floating up near the ceiling in the hallway and pushing myself around the low hanging lights. I assume I was on the verge of dying then.

Recuperating at home from Nephritis in 1959

31

Later in the summer, I took off down West Maple Street, again unsupervised, crossing streets and exploring. When I heard the screech of tires, I looked over and saw a little boy tumbling down the street. I sat on the curb and watched as his parents and the driver ran to him. A ball was in the street and I figured he'd run out into the street to fetch it and been hit. His forehead was all caved in and he was moaning. When the ambulance came, I ran home. I was scared and felt sad, but I didn't tell anyone what I saw because grown-ups usually didn't want to be bothered. In fact, there wasn't very much talking at all in our house.

August 1961

I started first grade at South Side Elementary in Johnson City, Tennessee. I was nervous that morning because Kenny said I'd get paddled if I talked. Mommy made me a blue satin dress to wear and braided my long hair. She walked me to school and I remember stepping through the front door and how it looked and smelled. It was a two-story building that seemed gigantic. My shoes clicked on the wooden floors. The smells were that wonderful childhood elixir of chalk, pencils and cafeteria food. The classrooms had huge windows. An upstairs window had a huge tube we would have to slide down on mats for fire drills. My classroom overlooked the playground where we would play cowboys and Indians during recess. Sometimes we found Indian arrowheads.

When school let out that first day, I waited on the steps for mommy to come for me, excited to tell her about my experiences. I waited and waited, but she didn't come. Finally, I slowly began walking the way I thought led towards home, looking for anything familiar. I wondered why mommy hadn't come and how she could have forgotten me.

Somehow I made it home and ran through the door and up the stairs. I put my hands on my hips and asked her why she didn't come and get me. Not looking at me, she shrugged and said she thought I knew how to get home. She didn't say anything else, so I went to my room, never telling her about my first day of school.

South Side Elementary before it was torn down

I was outside playing one day when Daddy came home from another out-of-town job. I ran to hug him and then, as he got his luggage out, ran upstairs to tell mommy that "daddy's home." She didn't look happy. "Aren't you glad daddy's home?" She mumbled yeah, but I knew she was lying. Somehow I sensed the bottom was about to fall out from under my safe world.

<u>June 1962, Queens, New York</u>

The summer after first grade we moved to Queens, New York. It was crowded and we mostly played on the sidewalk outside our apartment building. We went to Coney Island one day and I remember the giant wooden slides in Steeplechase and mommy and daddy riding on the parachute ride. As darkness fell and the crowd thinned out, I rode on the Ferris wheel with my older sister, Jean, and she fainted while we were on it. The last ride before we left for home was the Caterpillar. Mommy rode it with me, just the two of us. Nobody else was on the whole ride. As we flew around curves, the canopy covered us and mommy held me tightly and laughed. She seemed to be happy, but I found out, later on, she was happy because she had a secret, not because she was enjoying being with us.

I started second grade at PS 148. Before the year ended, we would move again, this time to Bensalem, Pennsylvania, an idyllic setting for the worst memories of my life.

Outside our home in Queens, New York

Chapter 2

Daddy's Legacy

<u>November 1962, 1515 Bristol Pike, Cornwell Heights,</u>
<u>Pennsylvania</u>

I *am eight years old and I live in a big, old Victorian house at 1515 Bristol Pike in Cornwell Heights (now Bensalem), Pennsylvania. I love the house with its nooks and crannies, the peaceful neighborhood with its big old homes, the woods we explore behind our house and the campus of Katherine Drexel convent a few blocks away. Everything here seems mysterious and magical. We live on the second and third floors and daddy's friend and coworker, Bill Brandon, lives on the first floor with his wife and two daughters. Bill had worked with daddy in Queens, too, and he has a trailer parked past the woods where mommy visits him sometimes.*

Behind the house is a dried up creek bed with a little wooden bridge. Kenny and I walk over it every day on our way to the woods to play. There is a little hole in the bridge where I dropped some seeds last night. I pretended the seeds would grow into a huge castle, with a handsome prince who would marry me and we'd live happily ever after. My prince would be just like my daddy.

Kenny and I have a secret clubhouse beneath a weeping willow tree and we let the Ivy brothers play with us there. They are closer to Kenny's age but they let me play with them, too.

Kenny and I watch television a lot. We especially love Twilight Zone. One episode was about a brother and sister, like us, only their parents would fight a lot. The kids found a crack in the pool bottom and swam through to a magical place where children are safe. When their parents didn't want to live together anymore, they asked the kids who they wanted to live with and the kids said, "Neither of you" and jumped in the pool. They went to the magical place and the crack closed up behind them. (Twilight Zone, 1964, The Bewitchin' Pool.)

Our neighborhood is beautiful and I love my friends, my school, my mommy and daddy, my Cocker Spaniel Mitsy and even my big brother Kenny. My daddy is my hero who can do no wrong and I just know he must be the strongest man in the world. I feel safe because he is like Superman and nothing can hurt me when he is around. If I am happy then surely mommy and daddy must be happy as well.

One night I was up in my bedroom playing with my pet caterpillar, Pinky. It was mommy and daddy's anniversary and the special cake mommy made was on the table. It had a little figure of a man and woman on it, the man on crutches made of toothpicks, because daddy had got hurt at work. Kenny was outside playing with the Ivy brothers. I heard someone yell, "The garage is on fire" and saw flashing lights through my window. I ran outside and watched as the firemen put out the fire. I was worried about Kenny, but then I saw him standing alone, looking scared, his bangs falling down over his eyes. The Ivy Brothers had run home. Kenny said they had been lighting matches and didn't mean to set a fire. Soon the fire was out, but some of our things were destroyed, including our swimming pool that had been with us through many years of moving around. I felt kind of sad, but was glad Kenny was okay.

***Our pool that got burned in the garage fire.
I would go underwater and peek out its
little window.***

I realized everyone else was back inside, so I climbed the stairs and the first thing I saw was the anniversary cake smashed on the floor. My sister, Jean, was staying with us because she was mad at her second husband. I asked her what happened and she said daddy knocked the cake off the table. I figured daddy must be really angry at Kenny so I ran to find him to see if he was okay. When I found him he said daddy did not yell at him, that something else was wrong, but nobody would tell me what happened. Everyone was quiet and nobody would talk to me, and I started rubbing my hand back and forth over my tummy, making a warm spot. Then I heard Kenny and Jean whispering about daddy finding a letter mommy was writing about taking a bath with Bill. She hid it behind the toilet when the fire started and daddy found it

Kenny had taught me about sex and we called it "bubbling". I knew mommy shouldn't be naked with anybody but daddy. I was scared and wondered what would happen now. Everybody seemed mad when I asked questions, even Dorothy, Bill's wife and their two daughters. It felt like something was my fault.

Mommy stopped eating and got so sick she went to the hospital. Daddy was quiet too, but he still sat by mommy's bedside when she came home, watching over her. Maybe he wasn't *too* mad at mommy.

Daddy's come in all sizes and some are jolly and some are quiet. They do all kinds of jobs and some are handy and some are not. My daddy is short, but to me he is the biggest and strongest man in the world. I love my daddy and I'll marry somebody just like him someday. I'm not afraid of him. I can ask him for things I want. He never spanks me or yells at me.

Everything changed that night. Daddy became moody, angry and critical. Blaming myself gave me a strange sort of control I reckon. If being bad had made this happen, then maybe being good could make things good again. I would be very good. Maybe daddy would notice me again and wouldn't be mad at me.

Most of my heartbreak in life involves men that I was not equipped to stand up to, starting with daddy. My daddy, my rescuer when I scraped a knee, my teacher when I wanted to learn to ride a bike, my indestructible, ever-present, dependable bulwark became overnight a weak, pitiful, angry soul that I feared, could no longer approach and, even more monumental, felt I had to take care of. Our roles were becoming reversed.

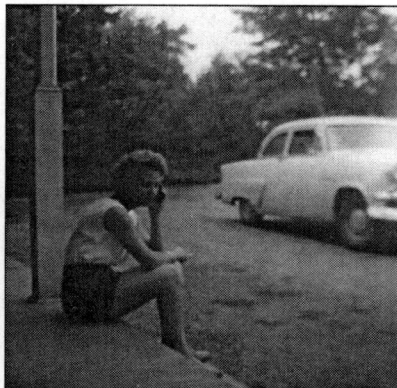

***Our house at 1515 Bristol Pike;
unhappy mom on the porch smoking***

My Worst Memory

Mommy broke daddy's heart and the hurt made him self-centered. He wanted the pain to end, being unable to see beyond it. Although I look back on him with pity, his next act was incredibly selfish because it ended childhood for his two youngest children.

Kenny and I were out playing beside the house when I noticed daddy sitting under a tree. It was odd to see daddy sitting on the ground, but I was happy, thinking he had come out to watch us play. I ran over to him excitedly, but seeing him up close stopped me in my tracks. I only remember a sense of horror and panic and then screaming to Kenny, "Something's wrong with daddy." The tone of my voice caused him to rush over and he saw daddy and turned from a boy into a man. Daddy's eyes were unfocused, rolling back in his head. He must have been sitting there for a few minutes before I noticed him because he couldn't have walked out in his condition. Memories are a blur until I stood beside his bed, the doctor putting his gear away, shaking his head and saying he felt sorry for daddy. And daddy was mumbling, "Help me, help me." I remember thinking that he must not really want to die or he wouldn't be asking for help.

Life is full of billions of memories with their sensations and feelings and I still feel many of them so deeply. But the worst memory of all is finding daddy under that tree, and then standing by his bedside after the doctor made him vomit up sleeping pills. I remember having an adult-like insight that daddy didn't really want to die and yet didn't want to live because mama had killed the part of him that a man just can't lose and go on living. I learned what a dilemma is without knowing the word. Daddy was emasculated, a shell, betrayed by a close friend and his wife. I also understood, on some deeper level, that he did not love his children enough to want to live and take care of us and that we really were not in the best of hands with mama either.

Daddy lived and life went on for a short time in that house. One morning I awoke to hear that Mitsy had "fallen" from the balcony. Mrs. Brandon had heard her crying outside her window and found her there, unable to get up. I still wonder how she got out on to the balcony and if she fell or someone dropped her over the side. Daddy insisted one of us sleep walked and let her out there. Kenny and I always wondered if daddy was so angry at us he took his rage out on Mitsy just to hurt us. Would daddy do that? It was no secret he thought pets were nasty. But would he try to kill our beloved pet, having not succeeded in taking his own life?

***Mom, me and Mitsy in the living room;
the balcony Mitsy "fell from"***

August 1963, 714 Clinton Avenue, Bucks County

We moved again to a house not too far away, but in a different school district. We called the empty lot next door "the swamp" because it was marshy, shady and cool. It was a great place to explore, probably home to dangerous snakes and brewing pools of disease. Mom and dad were in their own worlds so they never seemed to care where we were or what we were doing. I made friends in the neighborhood and it wasn't bad living there at first. Daddy made me water wings for our trip to the beach. Jean cut down one of her formal dresses so I could play dress up with it. The old man at the corner gave me treasures every time I went to see him. I put on boots and waded in the rain-filled ditches. And I learned to jump puddles on my bike. It was also where I lived when President Kennedy died and it was where daddy tried, for the second time, to die too.

Life became an unsettling routine of normalcy verses dysfunction. There were late night fights with mommy and daddy screaming downstairs.

"I'll stay with you, but I'll never sleep with you again."

"I can't live like that, without a man."

The fights left me terrified and I'd hold my stuffed animals and rock in the bed. I liked the little boy next door and I wondered if he could hear my parents fighting.

One night in the fall the house grew cold so daddy went down in the basement to investigate. I followed him, because I followed him everywhere, diligently trying to keep him safe. He took his crutch and poked at the furnace and suddenly flames shot out. He told me to get upstairs fast but I refused, thinking he might choose to stay down there and burn up. He couldn't walk fast on those crutches, but I refused to budge until he began hobbling up the steep staircase, following him as I fearfully looked back at that fire breathing monster. I knew since I was behind daddy I would take the brunt of an explosion. We made it upstairs and the fire trucks came and put out the fire, but we couldn't stay there without heat. We stayed in a hotel that night and, while we were gone, thieves burglarized our house.

A few nights later, daddy was up watching a ball game when I went to bed. I awoke in the middle of the night to a commotion and found daddy was lying in the yard where Kenny had dragged him. The garage door was open, but still smoky inside. Kenny said daddy asked him to bring his sleeping pill bottle, so Kenny got suspicious and tried to stay awake and watch him. He woke up a while later and went looking for daddy, finding him inside the car in the garage with the engine running and the door closed. The garage was so smoky he could hardly see, but he got the door open and got daddy out. Daddy was selfish for making Kenny get his pills, and the gas could have come in the house and killed us all.

The next day mommy said she needed to talk to Kenny and me about something:

"Your daddy needs to go the hospital because he keeps trying to kill himself. I don't want to make the decision to have him committed. I want you to tell me if you want him to go. But, you know, he really needs help and if he doesn't go, he might die. So now you two tell me what you want to do, because I'm not going to make the decision."

Naturally we agreed to it. I have never understood how she could manipulate her young children into making a decision that would follow us the rest of our lives. It was much too large a burden to place upon our small shoulders.

Daddy was so passive he didn't complain when the ambulance came for him. We stood in the yard when they wheeled him out and Jean commented, "I feel so sorry for him." I felt a tremendous weight of guilt and shame and wondered if she knew that it was our fault they were taking daddy away. I felt like a spotlight was shining on me because I had done this to him.

Later daddy would tell me how the other patients grabbed his strawberries. He was a picky eater and the strawberries were the only food he could eat there. He also said something about shock treatments. I carried guilt into adulthood when I would finally ask dad to forgive me. Even though he insisted it wasn't my fault, I needed to hear him say it.

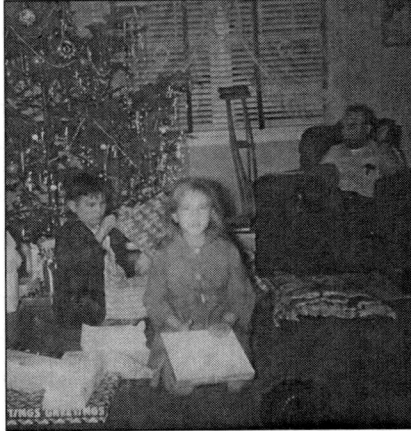

The living room of the 2nd Attempt House

Daddy's brothers drove in from Ohio to get daddy out of the hospital. Consequently, his second suicide attempt had further tragic ramifications, nearly causing the death of one of his brothers. Uncle Melvin was so tired after driving all night to get my daddy released, and having to get back to his city to work the next day, he fell asleep and hit a cattle truck so hard the truck turned over.

While daddy was away with his brothers, mommy wanted time alone with her boyfriend, so Jean and her husband took us to Wildwood to visit her husband's uncle near the ocean. Before we left, mommy modeled the dress she had made. It was blue and shiny and could be worn three ways. Mommy called it versatile. She looked beautiful with her blond curly hair. I liked it when mommy was happy because she paid more attention to me.

Jean's husband's uncle lived in a one bedroom trailer. Jean and her husband slept on the fold out sofa in the living room and Kenny and I slept with the uncle. When I woke up the next morning, the uncle's hand was in my panties and his finger was rubbing me inside. When I tried to turn away, he held me down with his hand. I was embarrassed, so I pretended to sleep. He finally stopped and I waited a minute and opened my eyes. He smiled at me and said good morning and I said good morning back. I told Kenny and, the next night, my sister made me sleep on a cot in the hallway. Men were so scary!

Back home, summer turned to autumn and school started again. On November 22, 1963 we got out of school early because of a blizzard. As we loaded the bus, I saw the driver crying. She told us President Kennedy had been shot and killed. When we got home mama was watching the TV and there was lots of news instead of the regular shows we watched. I felt sad because everyone loved President Kennedy and he was a good man.

One day I looked out my window and saw daddy walking down the street on his crutches, from the main road. He was back and the fights started again. I would often go to my room to listen to my records, trying to drown out their yelling. I would sing along with Lesley Warren "In my own little corner, in my own little chair, I can be whatever I want to be."[1]

A few nights later mommy was ironing and watching television when Marty Robbins came on, singing *El Paso*. Daddy walked in and hatefully said she only liked Marty Robbins so much because he looked like Bill Brandon.

August 1964, 2040 Street Road, Eddington, Bucks County

We moved into a third house, not too far away, and we had to change schools again. This was a pretty, old two-story farm house on acres of land with a large red barn. Kenny and I ran through the fields exploring old abandoned farm equipment. The house had a winding staircase and a scary basement we called the dungeon. Kenny and I spent a lot of time watching monster movies, like *The Creature from the Black Lagoon*, *Dracula* and *Frankenstein*. We collected monster cards that came in bubble gum packs. Even though we fought a lot, Kenny and I were close and we were a comfort to each other through all the bad times.

Kenny and I were sick a lot and he often had boils that had to be lanced. I can't remember mom ever making us brush our teeth or making us take regular baths. One morning I woke up with an awful toothache. It hurt so bad mommy let me stay home from school. I was miserable as I lay on the sofa, facing the back. Daddy walked up behind me and I hoped he was going to comfort me. Instead he yelled up the stairs to mommy, "She doesn't have a toothache, she just doesn't want to go to school, and you let her stay home just so you didn't have to be alone with me." I'm not sure which was worse, the pain in my mouth or the one in my heart.

One day Kenny and I were on the front porch when we saw Casey, mom's boyfriend, drive by and toot the horn. We waved at him and ran inside to tell mommy, then remembered that daddy was there and we had to keep it a secret. When daddy left again on another job, I came home from school one day and found mommy and Casey lying on the couch kissing.

September 1964, 1151 Wildman Avenue, Bucks County

I was only at school a couple of weeks when we moved again and I started yet another new school. Mommy was working at the State Hospital and daddy was mostly gone. When he was home, he slept in the attic. Mommy would make me take his supper up to him and I hated it because he wouldn't even look at me when I said softly,

"Daddy, here's your supper" and sat it down next to him. I would rush back downstairs afraid he would yell at me or knock the tray out of my hands. A part of me just wanted him to leave again so mommy would be happy and smile again.

One night I went with mommy into town. The car quit on the way and mommy pulled to the side of the road. She walked to a house and called Casey, because he owned a gas station and was a mechanic. Casey was looking under the hood when daddy pulled up behind us. Oh no, this wasn't good! I heard yelling and mommy got back in the car. Daddy followed us home and he and mommy started back yelling. Soon there was a knock at the door and Casey was standing there with his rifle. Daddy said, "Go ahead and shoot." I stood in front of the couch and watched, afraid to move. Was I finally going to see daddy die? Casey finally left and the next morning daddy did too.

I had been sleeping with mama and the next morning daddy woke me up to tell me goodbye. He bent over to hug me and I could feel his rough face and smell his daddy smell. He put mommy's diamond watch on my wrist, the one he'd bought mommy, because mommy had a bigger one that Casey had given her. I wish I could remember what daddy said to me before he left.

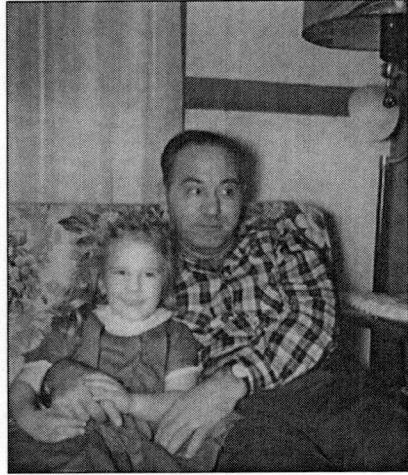

Posing for mom's ever-present camera;
in dad's lap as he watches the news

I'll Be Your Ballerina

(Written for daddy, but never given to him)
I'll be your ballerina if you'll be my shining prince,
my idol, whom I worship, without tarnish, without tints.
I'll dance for you and make you proud and be your little girl.
I'll dash and dart and pounce and bow and pirouette and twirl.
I'll look for you, my eyes will search, from up upon my stage.
The stars within my eyes will burn for none but you, my sage.
You are the first man in my life, the one I long to please.
You lift me on your shoulders, and with whiskered face you tease.
You hold my hands, my feet on yours, I walk upon your shoes.
I sit right down beside you while you watch the daily news.
I always feel so safe with you, just knowing you are near.
When I am with my daddy there's no reason to feel fear.
I'll dance for you, I'll twirl for you, I'll jump and twist and dive.
I'll be your ballerina if you'll please just stay alive.

Since daddy had left for good, mommy and Casey could date freely. Casey took us on a trip to Washington, DC and we got to see a museum with dinosaur bones and real planes and ships inside. He would take us to watch drag races, too. I liked going to his house and swimming in his pool. He was nice to mommy and to us. I guess he was still courting her, so he was on his best behavior. I'm thankful I was spared seeing him abuse her. Years later, I would be aware of the irony in the similarity between her situation and mine, the only difference being I would finally get away from my husband, but she stayed with Casey until he died many years later.

In Casey's pool; at the drag races; in Washington, DC.
Mom doesn't have her arms around me in either
picture where I'm cuddling up to her.

One morning daddy, Jean and her husband showed up at my school bus stop and told me to get in the car. Then we went to Kenny's junior high school and got him. We didn't go back to our house to get our clothes and toys, even though mommy was at work. We didn't get Mitsy either and she was, by far, more important than our toys and clothes. My brother and I were used to being passive observers in the drama of our lives. Neither of us spoke up to ask what would happen to us. We sat in the car silently, the miles taking us further and further from mommy. Daddy admitted later on we might have been better off with mom, and that he was using us as weapons to hurt her, but life with her and Casey wouldn't have been good either.

Mom's new, sad reality. Her kids were gone and Casey used her for a punching bag.

Halloween, October 1964, Johnson City, Tennessee

Daddy took Kenny and me to grandma's house where we would live with grandma, grandpa and my Aunt Violet. It was Halloween and my cousins were coming over to trick or treat with us that night. Kenny opted out, thinking he was too old, and I didn't have a costume since we had just arrived that day. Someone had one of those eye masks for me, so I went out in the school dress I'd had on that morning in Pennsylvania. I joined a group of other children who were all wearing elaborate costumes. At one house a nice lady opened the door, her eyes taking us all in. Her eyes stopped at me and she said, "Oh, don't you look so pretty in your dress and mask. What a pretty little girl!" I glowed, even though I knew she was just going out of her way to be nice because I didn't have a costume.

For a few weeks, while daddy was there, we were treated well, even pampered. But the novelty wore off soon and it became clear that we were an inconvenience, a fact that was not hidden from us. My aunt demonstrated her annoyance almost daily through things she would say to me, and in her mannerisms. Kenny was older and spent a lot of time away from home, so she didn't say much to him. I felt intimidated by my aunt and tried hard to please her and make her like me.

One Sunday daddy was leaving for the week. I didn't want him to go because I knew my aunt would treat me differently once he left. As he walked down the long stairway to the sidewalk, I began to cry. He looked back and waved at me, but I couldn't stop crying. Suddenly I heard my aunt's voice behind me. "You should be ashamed for making your daddy worry about you like that. He works hard for you and now he'll be worried about you being sad instead of thinking about his driving and his work, and he might get hurt." She had touched a sensitive nerve by talking about daddy getting hurt and my "protect daddy" mode kicked in, along with heaps of guilt and shame. I also wanted to please her, so I quickly wiped my eyes, forced a smile and called out, "Daddy, be careful. I love you." Daddy smiled, looking relieved, and got in his car and left. I had saved my daddy again.

I missed mommy so badly. Some nights I dreamed about her and usually, when I did, she would call the next day. I was always happy when I dreamed about her because I figured I'd get to talk to her. My cousin, Larry, thinks that he and I have a bit of "the sight", the ability to sense things before they happen, a characteristic that supposedly runs in some hillbilly families.

Casey tried taking me out of school one day, so daddy figured he'd better get legal custody of us. He found a lawyer and a trial date was set. He asked me to tell the judge all of mama's boyfriends' names. Judges are really scary. Mommy didn't show up for the hearing. She claimed she never got the notice, but I found it in some papers she gave me when I was an adult.

Once daddy had formal custody, he let me see mama when she came to town. One day she picked me up for the day and we went to a lawyer's office where she asked if there was a way she could still get custody. I guess the lawyer told her she'd stand a better chance if she could get me back to Pennsylvania. When he asked if I wanted to live with mommy, I said yes. After all, nobody in Johnson City really wanted me.

Mommy met Kenny and daddy in the Dairy Queen parking lot that night to hand me back over. But instead of handing me over she told daddy I wanted to go live with her. She reached for me and I went into her arms and then Kenny and daddy grabbed me by the feet to pull me into their car. Mommy had my arms now, trying to pull me into her car, and I was getting stretched in two directions. I started crying because I really wanted them both. Daddy and Kenny won the tug-o-war and got me in the car and they took me over to Aunt Dee's house.

At Aunt Dee's I went down in the basement to play with my cousins. I heard my name called and looked up to see Violet's adult daughter at the top of the steps. She had her hands on her hips and was shaking her head. "Anna, you ought to be ashamed, hurting your daddy like that. How could you want to leave him and go live with your mama after the way she treated him? I can't believe you'd do that to him." I hung my head and felt like I had failed daddy again, but I just wanted mommy. After all, all my cousins had their mommies.

One day, when I was twelve, I stood in grandma's back porch thinking about God, wondering why He didn't reveal Himself more to us. Kenny had told daddy how Aunt Violet treated me, so daddy moved me in with a lady he was dating. I went to church with her on Sundays, to an Apostolic Church. Everyone prayed out loud at one time there, and people lifted their hands and praised God. Sometimes they prayed in different languages that sounded beautiful. One day a man spoke in a different language and then another man interpreted it. I was so happy I got goosebumps all over, realizing that God *does* speak to us. He's closer to us than I ever knew He was!

When daddy broke up with his girlfriend, I was back at grandma's house again. I started seventh grade at South Junior High School when I was twelve. It was another great, old building that has since been torn down.

South Junior High School

When Jean broke up with her husband for good, daddy bought a trailer so we could all four live in it and Jean could watch us when he was gone on jobs. He parked it in a little trailer park in Johnson City. I liked it because I was with Kenny and Jean and we lived close to most of my relatives. We were living there when I turned thirteen. Right before my birthday mama left Casey and was in town staying with her parents. I invited her over to our trailer to help me celebrate. Putting some records on to play, I pulled daddy out of his bedroom and insisted he dance with mom. As they awkwardly danced, I dreamed of them getting back together.

With mom when I turned thirteen.

Before mom left that night, she offered me a precious doll from her collection. I knew she valued her dolls and I felt honored and special. It didn't matter that I didn't play with dolls anymore.

The next day daddy let me go over to visit mom for a while at my maternal grandparents' cabin. Mom said she had been feeling poorly and that she needed to talk to me. I had a feeling I was not going to like what she had to say. "I was pregnant," she confessed. "It was a little girl and Casey was excited and told me he hoped she would look just like me." She told me she lost the baby and that Casey would blame her for it because she made the long trip from Pennsylvania, where they still lived, down to Johnson City. I felt betrayed that she almost let another little girl replace me and I could tell, from the way she was talking, she was going to go back to Casey. When mama took me back home later, she asked if she could borrow the doll she had given me. I ran inside to get it and handed it to her as she hugged me and told me she'd see me the next day. But the next day she was gone, as she knew she would be, with the doll she had given me. She left without saying goodbye.

Jean met husband number three and was going to move out, so when daddy took a job in Mooresville, North Carolina he made plans to get the trailer moved there so he could take me too. Kenny was graduating high school soon and he had his own car, so he would move back in to grandma's house. For a time I had enjoyed the stability of being around family and attending the same school. But now, as a teenager, I would have to transfer to a new school in yet another strange town. And it would be just me and my dad.

Chapter 3

A New Mom

Fall 1969, Mooresville, North Carolina

I really missed Kenny and I was lonely because dad and I rarely talked. We spent most of our time reading or watching television. One night, during a commercial, I asked him, "Daddy, do you think I'm beautiful?" Daddy prided himself on his honesty. He minced no words this time, as usual. "Ahhh, well, you're okay." It wouldn't have hurt him to say, "Honey, you're beautiful to me" and to explain that what's on the inside is most important. His response crushed me and I remember thinking that, since daddy wouldn't lie, I was not even pretty. How would anyone ever want me?

Daddy didn't know how to pick out clothes for me, so I picked out whatever I wanted. My hair was long, hanging over my eyes and I didn't know how to properly use make up. I felt ugly and I think I tried to hide my face behind my hair. I was painfully shy and withdrawn and rarely talked to anyone at school. Some of the girls were rough and tried to pick fights with me. I tried to put on a tough demeanor, but inside I was trembling. Sometimes daddy would leave

57

for work and I would skip school, writing my own sick notes. For the first time, I failed a grade.

Daddy decided I needed a mother so he joined a matchmaker service, asking for a lady who didn't smoke and who liked opera. He was matched with a lady in South Carolina who smoked and hated opera. He drove to her house to meet her one Saturday, leaving me home alone. I guess he liked her because the next trip he took me to meet her. It didn't take him long to ask Geraldine to marry him. She accepted and I soon found myself with a stepmom. She had two grown children, a son and daughter, with children of their own.

I'm not sure what Geraldine thought of me, but I was thrilled to have her around. I didn't have to be daddy's guardian or help plan meals. And I longed for someone's guidance as I grew into a woman. The three of us would play cards together at night, listening to Jim Reeves records. She was a strong-willed woman and sometimes openly critical to dad, but I grew to love her very much through the years, and she taught me a lot about life and how to behave properly.

With Geraldine and Dad

August 1970, Rome, Georgia

Things were great for a while, as I basked in the attention my stepmom gave me. Despite a few teenage uprisings, we got along great. We moved to Rome, Georgia, where I repeated eighth grade, her helping me study each night. This time I got straight A's. I even wrote a whole book for a writing assignment. I titled it "Red" and it was about a Russian invasion of America. My teacher was so impressed he said to use him for a college reference. My stepmom helped me shop for clothes and get my hair styled. Each night we would exercise in the living room, laughing at each other when we lost our balance while doing bicycles.

June 1971 – August 1972, Liberty, South Carolina

Daddy was soon transferred again, but this time he and my stepmom decided to leave me with my stepsister, Linda, her husband and their two little boys. I started ninth grade at Liberty High School and attended church at their church, the Liberty Church of God, a Pentecostal church. It wasn't a shock to me since I'd been exposed to Pentecostalism before. This time I was older and took more of an interest. The worship was meaningful and God's presence was very real. I began seeking the Baptism of the Holy Spirit, as it is referred to in the New Testament. I gladly accepted and adhered to the church's strict teachings because I longed to feel loved by God. Unfortunately, I felt I had to gain His approval by dressing a certain way and adhering to our church's rules or "Practical Commitments".

I was happy with Linda but my stable life was not to be. Dad and my stepmom decided I needed to live with them again. When they picked me up from Linda's house, I was crying and my stepmom told me I looked like a mule with my long hair, long dress and my long, pouting face. The rapport we had enjoyed in the past was gone because I had embraced the church and she was at odds with their teachings. Sadly, a chasm was born between us that would not heal for many years. I never suspected she was trying to hurt me on purpose, but I did feel that she might unintentionally give me bad spiritual advice because she was "not right with God". We had a constant battle, her trying to get me to shorten my dresses and wear make-up, and my wanting to live how the church told me I should. No one knew, until many years later, that at this time she was in the beginning stages of Alzheimer's and it could have contributed to her suspicions and her critical nature.

Late August 1972, Copperhill, Tennessee and McCayesville, Georgia

I started the next school year in Copperhill, Tennessee, but would only be there a short time. The apartment we lived in was not satisfactory so we moved a few blocks away into a house, which put us over the state line in to McCayesville, Georgia. I transferred to a new school yet again. I was close enough to the Church of God, however, that I could walk to church.

While living in McCayesville I became plagued with nightmares. They all had the same theme of my being blamed for things I didn't do. I feel certain it was my emotional suffering over my stepmom's dissatisfaction with me and my desire to be accepted by both God and her. I was a typical teen with my own unique quirks, but she often made remarks that caused me to feel something was wrong with me, such as telling me I was mentally slow. That would stay with me even when I graduated summa cum laude from graduate school.

One morning I sat on the side of the bed and felt a whistling in my ears, then fainted and hit the floor. My stepmom kept me home that day and took me to the doctor, telling him how I liked to fast and pray. He told her to leave me alone and let me fast and be thankful I was a good girl that gave her no problems. I needed thyroid medication for a while and never fainted again.

The Comfort of God

One weekend we went to Johnson City to see my grandparents. Ever the faithful one, I would not miss church service so, Sunday morning, I walked to the nearby Church of God I always visited while in town. In Sunday School I felt God's Spirit especially strong and felt something exciting was happening in my life. That night, back in my church in McCayesville, I went to the altar at the end of the service. One moment I was praising God with all my heart, trying to tell Him how much I loved Him, and the next thing I knew I was on my knees still praising God but the words were not my own. My own vocabulary had reached its limits in expressing what I was trying to communicate to God. The Holy Spirit, Who "searches the heart and mind" (Romans 8:26, 27) was expressing to God what I could not adequately say. Wow, this was cool! God was with me and loved me. I wasn't alone. Unfortunately, He didn't automatically infuse me with wisdom, like Solomon. I had much to learn. When I got home, my stepmom chided me for being late. "Blame God," I told her. Yep, I could have been a lot more diplomatic! I came to understand that mom was actually feeling sad and convicted because she was longing for the relationship with God that I had. The church had failed her years before, when she tried to live according to their strict teachings, but couldn't afford new clothes that would meet their modest dress requirements. She was raising her two children by herself on wages from a cotton mill. She was still hurting from the insensitivity of the church.

October 1972 – August, 1973, Rogersville, Tennessee and Johnson City, Tennessee

We moved mid-school year again to Rogersville, Tennessee and I finished the eleventh grade, lacking only one credit of Senior English to graduate. That summer I moved back in with my grandparents in Johnson City and took my final unit of Senior English at East Tennessee State University's University High School. Then I got a job in a nearby sewing factory and pondered what to do with my life. Dad and my stepmom offered to pay my way through nursing school, but I didn't pass the interview. My stepmom asked if I'd like to move in with her son's family in Piedmont, South Carolina, not far from Linda's house, until I figured out what I wanted to do.

1974 – 1977, Liberty, South Carolina

I only lived with my stepbrother a short time. I had felt more comfortable with Linda, so I soon moved back in with her and got a job at a piano factory. My stepmom was not happy with this situation. I remember well the day she told Linda that I needed guidance, being like a child. "What are you going to do when she tells you she wants to go screw some boy in the middle of the street?" My heart was broken. I would never want to do something like that. My stepmom did not know I had an inner strength and that I was a good girl. She expected me to act out like my siblings had done, rather than judging me on my own merits and trusting my maturity. She suspected my loyalty to dad, thinking I just wanted what he could give me materially. All I ever really wanted from her and dad was acceptance and love.

When dad retired, they moved the trailer down the street from Linda. Dad extended the side of it, making it look more like a house. Linda had the same issue I had in the past of fearing her mom would, unintentionally, be a bad spiritual influence, so she did not let her children stay with dad and her mom as much as my stepmom wished. My stepmom suspected I was trying to turn Linda against her and that I was trying to come between her and my dad. In reality I was over-joyed that dad had her, and I never tried to influence Linda to keep her children away from them. My impression was that my stepmom was jealous because Linda and I were so close. I think she felt hurt and left out. I began to suspect that perhaps they would get closer if I was not around.

I loved being with Linda's family and her sons were like my own little brothers. I didn't like feeling, however, that I was causing problems for everyone, and I wanted something more out of life. I wanted to be in ministry. When my stepmother asked me to stop calling her "mom", I was hurt and just wanted to get out of everyone's way. My self-sacrificial little Anna had surfaced again, putting everyone else's needs first instead of staying and fighting for myself.

One day at work I was feeling particularly sad about my step-mom's rejection. It was not in my nature to fight back or feel angry at someone, so I punished myself instead. I went to the restroom with a safety pin and scratched my arm up. Somehow it helped get my focus off of my incredible load of mental confusion and pain. I had scratched my boyfriend's initials into my leg as a teenager, after hearing about other friends doing it, but this scratching had a different motivation. I wore long sleeves until it healed so no one would see.

I was trying to figure out how to get out of Liberty when I heard that our church's affiliated college in Cleveland, Tennessee was having College Day. I signed up to go, thinking I might pursue a career in Christian Education since I loved working with children so much. When the day arrived, I got on the bus at our Church of God State Headquarters and headed toward Cleveland, Tennessee.

PART II

...Make Older Victims

Every time we impose our will on another,
it is an act of violence–Ghandi

*The face of abuse, near the end of my bondage. After we had
lived with her nearly a decade, George's mom snapped this
picture after one of George's tirades. Then she told me to look at
myself and announced I had her blessing to find someone else to
love. Seeing the misery on my face was sobering.*

Chapter 4

Lee College

September 1977 – June 1983, Cleveland, Tennessee

*W*hile I loved the church and how it brought me to a closer walk with God, I was beginning to question some of the teachings. I sought out the advice of a couple who would become my "spiritual parents", Jere and Sue. Sue was a pastor's daughter and had, therefore, grown up in the church, yet she wore her hair short, used makeup and even wore jewelry and slacks. She genuinely loved God and I envied her independent attitude. God was working in my life in several ways: using family circumstances to nudge me out on my own; helping me use my own mind to formulate sound spiritual decisions; and placing me in an environment where I would begin to examine my past and its influence. I was extremely naïve about life, God and men. The road ahead would be a long and difficult one. I wanted to be in ministry, but sometimes ministering takes a road we would never consciously choose.

I applied to Lee College (now Lee University) and was accepted. In September 1977, at 22 years of age, I left Liberty, South Carolina

67

with only a couple of boxes of possessions. I had sold my car, so Jere and Sue drove me to the campus and settled me in at the freshmen Simmons Hall. Most of the girls were just out of high school and seemed happy and excited to be away from home. I was shy, scared and terribly self-conscious. I doubted my ability to make it and felt cut off from church and family support.

I soon settled in to the routine of classes, studying, going to the cafeteria for meals, and making some new friends. I made good grades and worked as many hours as I could on work study, so I could afford laundry and personal items. Sue often sent me a small check to help out, or outfits that she had made me. I felt blessed to have her and Jere on my side, wanting me to succeed. I had spent most of my pay, while living at home, on children's church items. Now my home church purchased my books for me one or two semesters. When I found out some people in the church were offended by that, I told them I no longer needed their help.

A few guys on campus told me, later on, they wanted to ask me out, but thought I was stuck up because I wouldn't look at them when I passed them on campus. I had hardly dated and felt uncomfortable around men and couldn't look a boy in the face when I did go out with him.

I found comfort in my times of prayer, learning more about the Holy Spirit and His role as intercessor. Many people who have not experienced the prayer language of the Holy Spirit think it is strange and some even liken it with some type of ungodly "possession". Other denominations claim that the Baptism of the Holy Spirit was only for the early church. This keeps them from having to deal with an uncomfortable issue. An open-minded approach to scripture, as well as authentic searching in prayer with an open heart, can clarify misconceptions. It is also helpful to realize that the Holy Spirit knows no church borders. I have charismatic friends in many Protestant denominations and even in the Catholic Church. I recommend a book written by a skeptical and critical truth-seeker John Sherrill (*They Speak with Other Tongues*) which has been in print for many years.

George

At the end of the winter semester, having nowhere to go, I opted to take General Psychology during the summer session. The instructor was also the director of the Counseling Center on campus. Another person opted to take the same class that summer. His name was George and he caught my eye immediately. For one thing, he wasn't younger than I. He was also nice looking in a kind of European way. He had a full beard, thick, dark, wavy hair and dark brown eyes. He was short, slim and very neat and clean. After seeing my high grades, he asked me to help him study.

George had his eye on another girl on campus, plus he was still under the spell of a girl back home, Sarah. He eventually noticed me more, but sadly I would be his third choice and I settled for that. Like other guys on campus, he thought I was stuck up because I was shy. His perception changed one night when I agreed to swim in the bubbling fountain in front of the Administration Building.

General Psychology class had me pondering my tattered emotions and fear of the future. I mentioned that to my professor and he suggested I keep a "thought journal" and then come in to talk with him. It was embarrassing opening up to a man, and I couldn't show emotion in front of him. Seeing a mouse in his office one day, I chose to ignore it and, when he saw it a few minutes later and warned me,

I told him I had seen it. He was amazed. "Anna, do you know that when you talk about how people have hurt you, you keep a smile on your face? Why do you hide your emotions?" I couldn't answer him. I had noticed that whenever anger welled up in me, it would suddenly just disappear before I could express it. I didn't understand that there hadn't been room for me to show emotions, nor had it been safe to do so. Everyone else's problems had taken precedence. Whereas some kids act out when they want attention, I just tried to fade in to the background and be good.

In one session I revealed that I felt so alone I was afraid I'd marry the first man who asked me. A couple of months later George and I passed the counselor on the sidewalk. George noticeably changed his voice to a much deeper tone before they greeted each other, which I thought was odd and perhaps an indication of masculine insecurity. For a moment a part of me cried out to the counselor in my mind, "Something feels wrong about this. Please counsel me. Tell me if I'm doing the wrong thing and if I'm with the wrong man for me." I ignored that inner voice, thinking I was overly cautious. After all, other girls on campus constantly came up to me and told me how lucky I was to have found such a nice guy, like George. When George finally felt convinced God would allow him to marry, he proposed to me. I accepted and thought I was happy, but I know I had a nagging impression that something might not be right.

The Wedding

That summer George showed me the upstairs apartment he had rented for us in an old house not too far from campus. Before walking me back to campus, he stood in front of me and said, "I asked God to send someone that I could fall in love with the Christ in her and she could fall in love with the Christ in me. I'm going to learn so much from you." In the coming years, I would recall that he said nothing about what he wanted to offer me. I only remember thinking if he loved Christ that much, surely this would work out fine.

On May 11, 1979 we married in my home church in Liberty, South Carolina. I was a 24 year old virgin who had rarely dated and had grown up without any significant female or male guidance. My church family expected great things for me. I was marrying a future minister and would probably be a preacher's wife someday. The whole church showed up and I looked ahead with anticipation, although a bit of anxiety about the wedding night. I had no reason to fear George yet. After all, he was a Christian and Christian men should be safe, right?

When I observe other couples anticipating their weddings now, I realize how terribly wrong our situation was. George was worried up until the last moment that he was not doing God's will. Rather than thanking God for bringing him his soul mate, he was insecure and anxious. I'm sure he was comparing me to Sarah. His insecurity was nagging at me, but I assumed it was not unusual. Since I'd never been made to feel special, I didn't understand that his demeanor with me was abnormal.

We couldn't afford a honeymoon so, after the reception, we headed back to Cleveland in a car loaned to us by our best man and maid of honor, Amos and Julie. In the car, George rubbed my breasts and I felt anxious about what was to come. I knew George had been with other women and wondered how I would measure up. I had saved my precious gift of virginity for this man and I wanted him to be pleased with me.

I'd like to say the wedding night was enjoyable, but it wasn't. I was awkward and I think I was the first virgin he'd ever had. It seemed he expected me to know what to do, and I was looking to him for guidance. There was no cuddling afterward and I felt let down.

His True Colors

Our first grocery shopping trip, the next morning, was sobering since neither of us expected it to be so expensive. I was excited about cooking meals for my new husband. Again wanting to impress him, I arose early the next morning and made him healthy baked oatmeal with nuts, raisins and cinnamon. I popped it in the oven and sliced some strawberries. I had just started sprinkling a little sugar over them when George walked in to the kitchen.

"Good morning," I said, smiling at him.

He didn't answer and he didn't look happy. In fact, he looked miserable. Then he watched me for a second before yelling hatefully, "What are you doing?"

I almost dropped the sugar bowl. "I'm sweetening the strawberries."

"You ruined them. They don't need sugar." Banging his fist on the counter he told me he didn't want any of them, that I could eat them all.

"I'm sorry," I quickly said. "My family always added some sugar. I'll rinse them off."

"Don't bother. I said I didn't want any. You eat them."

Tears stung my eyes as I put the berries away. The oatmeal was beginning to smell good and I waited for it to finish, afraid to leave the kitchen. I was too shocked to move, other than to dry the tears off my cheeks. I wondered if he was already displeased with me and if he was regretting our marriage. "I must have really disappointed him last night," I thought.

I could hear him getting dressed in the bedroom and then walking to the living room. I placed the oatmeal at our settings and went to call him to eat. The neighbors had given us some old furniture and he was sitting on the sofa staring off in space. I timidly told him breakfast was ready. I walked in ahead of him then turned around, hopefully, as he looked at the meal. "What is this?" he demanded.

"It's baked oatmeal. It's very healthy."

"Why didn't you just make plain oatmeal? I don't need all that crap you put in it. I don't want it. You eat it. And eat it all. I don't want to see it wasted. It cost too much money." Then he got up and went back into the living room.

I couldn't understand his violent reaction. All he had to do was tell me what he wanted and I'd make it for him. This time I followed him into the living room.

"But what will you eat? You'll be hungry."

His response was to take off his wedding band and hurl it across the room. Then he stormed out and I heard him descending the steps outside.

I threw out the oatmeal, already deciding I'd tell him I had eaten it. Our second day of marriage and the part of me who valued honesty was manufacturing lies! "He must hate me. Maybe he hates how my body looks or is disappointed with the sex. Maybe he has realized I'm just not pretty enough for him." My mind went in a vicious circle, trying to make sense of it all.

I kept thinking of how angry he had looked with his face red, veins bulging in his neck and forehead, and strange cat-like eyes with elongated pupils. His fists had been balled up and spit had flown out of his mouth. He'd stood very close to me and I realized that I had been afraid, cringing and bracing, expecting he might hit me.

I sank down in the kitchen chair and started bawling. "What am I supposed to do now? I gave him my virginity, pledged myself to him for life. Is this normal? Is this how all men are?"

My eyes were red when he returned. "What's wrong?" he asked.

"You're mad at me and I don't know why."

"Well don't put sugar on anything and just cook plain oatmeal from now on."

"Okay," I said. I couldn't remember ever feeling so miserable.

That night when he made love to me he became impatient. "You're not moving right. Move with me, not against me." I'd try to change my rhythm, but when I did he changed his and he yelled at me again. By the time we were done, I was feeling like I would never get sex right. When I sensed he was sleeping, I got out of bed and sat in front of the open window, looking up through the tree at the summer sky and quietly crying.

"What's wrong with you?" he hatefully asked, startling me.

Too scared to be truthful, I told him, "I'm just praying." I think he knew I was lying, but didn't care, turning over and ignoring me. I felt my world was ending. With shame, I realized how easily I had lied when he asked, after sex, if I had "come". I had prided myself in being honest, but now was beginning to sacrifice my convictions along with my identity.

A Normal Dysfunction

The first time he lost his temper I was in shock and I sometimes think I never came out of it. It was like living under the shadow of an active volcano and wondering when the next eruption would occur. He would throw chairs and scream, making me wonder what the lady downstairs thought about the noise.

I continually questioned my own actions and tried to learn to think before I acted or spoke. I walked on egg shells when he was home. My stomach hurt constantly. Food seemed to go right through me, making me run to the bathroom with diarrhea. In our small apartment it was impossible to hide the noises my body made as it released everything I had eaten over the last day. I could hear him grumbling in annoyance and disgust and I dreaded walking out of the bathroom. When I did, he was standing there glaring at me. "Did you spray? It stinks in there." My face was flushed with embarrassment and, as he stormed out of the apartment to escape his disgusting wife, I suddenly had the urge to punish myself for being so ugly, disgusting and *wrong*.

Along with my college education I was learning to cope with my new life. I laughed to myself bitterly, thinking I could start a book, "Survival Tactics for Stupid Wives: 101" filled with wisdom I had garnered, such as: I would hold my bowel movements until he was in the shower. Then I would take an empty throw-away container, go to the bedroom, poop in it and run it out to the trash. He took very long showers, so I never got caught. I learned to run every menu by him before I planned meals, creating a week's menu ahead of time. I learned how to have dinner ready precisely at 6:00, not a minute before or after. I learned to quietly clean up broken dishes from the sink or off the floor where he'd thrown them. I learned to quickly paste a smile on my face if someone came to the door and that very cold water can hide the redness of eyes swollen from crying. And I learned how to think up lies quickly.

Why didn't I leave right then? I didn't know this was abnormal. I didn't know if I could go to heaven if I divorced. I was terribly naïve, and I had been made to feel stupid before I was old enough to realize I didn't have to believe what I was told about myself. I was in shock, finding it difficult to accept this was actually happening. Life felt surreal. I felt numb at times, dissociated from what was happening, listening to him yelling in my face, but feeling like I wasn't really there. I couldn't be. I couldn't have messed up my life this badly. Surely he was going through some phase and would calm down. He had been so charming and thoughtful when we were dating. I had given him my virginity and now I was no good to anyone else. I wasn't sure a divorcee could move back on campus and I could never afford an apartment on my own. I didn't want to disappoint my church family, who had put so much hope in me. I couldn't be in ministry if I was divorced, could I?

I could almost picture my stepmom shaking her head knowingly, saying to me, as she had to Linda, "You made your bed now lay in it." There was just too much to think about. I felt dizzy and overwhelmed when I thought about trying to leave. I had a full time class load and a work-study job.

I felt guilty because I had wanted this man and had thought I couldn't live without him. I had cried out to God, begging Him to let me finally find somebody to love me so I wouldn't have to feel so alone. I felt I had no right to complain to God because He had given me what I so badly wanted. I could almost picture God shaking His head, chiding me, "This is what you asked for because you wouldn't trust Me to send you the right person. You made your bed and now you have to lay in it."

I had hinted to a classmate what was happening and her advice had been to fulfill my role as a supportive, obedient Christian wife and he would automatically fulfill his role. I fulfilled my role and kept waiting, but he never did.

I'm not sure which I dreaded most, his angry tirades or his sullen silences. I became adept at reading his moods, his actions, and his expressions, and recognized a pattern. There was usually a long bout of silence followed by an explosion. If he shaved his beard off, it meant a good mood for the day, or at least a few hours, because he thought that the change in his appearance would magically cause a change in his life. I worked hard for the rare moments he laughed and smiled and gave me a little attention, so-called "honeymoon periods". I coveted times other students would be around because I knew he would never act out in front of someone else and I would be safe as long as people were around.

I learned it was not a good idea to ever offer my opinion, but to just be agreeable. I must have wished, a thousand times, I could go back in time one hour or one minute and do something differently, thinking I could change his demeanor with my actions.

He told me what to eat and how much, what to wear, how to style my hair, what books I should and shouldn't read and even how to walk. I had dreamed of being beautiful to the man I married and tried my best to please him, but my attempts were met with hostility and suspicion. Nothing I did was ever enough. Anger seemed to be his normal and first reaction to anything. It reminded me of a child throwing a tantrum; only in an adult it's so obscene it's terrifying. Crying got me no sympathy and there were never any apologies.

One night we were sitting in a pew waiting for church to start, and I laughed at something he said. He hesitated, looking at me, and I tensed up. Then he surprised me, saying, "I'd miss your laugh if you were gone." It was the first hint he'd ever given me that he might be glad to have me around, and this was probably months or maybe even a year in to our marriage. It was like throwing a crumb to a starving dog. My heart lifted and my hope soared. Maybe he was changing. Maybe God was answering my prayer and having mercy on me. Maybe my husband was finally starting to like me.

Unfortunately, his bizarre behavior did not change. The next day he told me to stop wearing silky lingerie on Sundays, because we shouldn't have sex on *The Lord's Day* anymore. I got the impression that he felt sex was somehow sinful, dirty or displeasing to God. The same day he broke two photos taken of him in a car race. He seemed to believe his destroying them was a symbolic gesture of walking away from his past, a sacrifice to earn God's favor.

I decided to seek council from a pastor at North Cleveland Church of God, the largest Church of God in Cleveland, which was within walking distance of our apartment. I was shown in to a co-pastor's office and began telling him about George's behavior. He said I should have the marriage annulled, telling me something was drastically wrong with George. When I voiced my fear of offending God, he said in Christ's day divorce was a game where men would marry and divorce on a whim. If a man got tired of his wife or saw someone he liked better, he could just say "I divorce you" and go on to the next one. He insisted I had legitimate grounds to leave George, however I was thinking that an annulment would not give me back my virginity.

I was not ready to give up on my marriage but I knew I needed to confront George about his behavior. Terrified of trying to talk to George, I asked a pastor friend, who was aware of George's behavior, to confront him for me. He agreed and, as the time approached, I felt sick with fear. *The pastor never showed up*, telling me the next day he had feared George's reaction. He encouraged me to give it a little more time while his church prayed for my situation.

Timidly, I told George I'd heard someone say it was not sinful to have sex on Sunday. He demanded to know who I had talked to. I said I'd heard it in my ethics class, but he suspected I had talked to someone. "You can't trust counselors or doctors," he informed me. "You have God's word and that's all you need to know what's right and wrong. And you can always ask me if you have a question."

Sex was a dreaded experience, nothing like I had dreamed of. I was amazed he couldn't tell I didn't enjoy it. I was quiet, unresponsive and only touched him if he asked me to because he didn't like being touched. If I was on top, I had to make sure my long hair didn't fall into his face. I remember thinking of those stupid books and movies where the man likes it when his wife's hair falls over his face. I was learning bitter lessons about the real world. As he pounded into me tears ran down my cheeks, making me thankful the room was dark because my tears always angered him. I would pray desperately in my mind, "Please God, let him finish."

After sex George always rushed to the bathroom to repeatedly scrub his hands, his penis and to wash out his mouth, rinsing and spitting repeatedly. Then he'd come back to bed and turn his back to me without saying a word. I would also turn my back to him, so that I wouldn't breathe on him because he didn't like that. If I was really tired and breathed heavily in my sleep, he would wake me up, yelling and startling me. I can still hear his words, sometimes accompanied by a fist pounding the mattress, "Anna, you're breathing heavy!" Then I'd lay awake, concerned that I'd start breathing heavily again if I fell asleep.

Carroll Court

We were eventually accepted into the married housing unit, Carroll Court, and moved into our new apartment. I hoped I would feel less alone and a bit more safe in close proximity to other couples. My first memory of our moving in adventure was him yelling at me that I was stupid because I wasn't holding something right for him to nail down. It only made things worse because my hands would shake and my eyes would get watery and I couldn't really see what I was doing. Although he wasn't actually hitting me, his words were like physical blows. They came quickly and unexpectedly, sometimes because I couldn't read his mind and know what he wanted me to do. For years, I would cringe when anyone in authority asked me to help with a task. I wondered if the couples in nearby apartments could hear his shouting.

Brush with Death? (Ted Bundy)

One day after class I headed for the parking lot where a man was working on a white Volkswagen near my car. He asked me to sit in the driver's seat and push the brake pedal. I noticed the passenger seat was missing and that the guy was lying on the ground peering up at me. I hadn't put both feet in, feeling vulnerable, and I thought he was trying to look up my skirt. I got out quickly and thankfully saw George coming down the sidewalk with a classmate. I waved at him, informing the man my husband was coming and he would help. Years later, when I saw Ted Bundy's car in a movie, I got goosebumps, realizing it could have well been him. When they showed a picture of the real killer, it looked like the man who had asked me for help. I wondered if it was him and if so, did God spare me for some purpose.

**Ted Bundy's famous Volkswagen,
identical to the one I sat in.**

Fury on the Atlanta Bypass

At semester's end, we got up at midnight and headed down to Fort Lauderdale to spend Christmas with George's mom. As we approached Atlanta, I was helping him watch for exits. Apparently I pointed to the bypass exit when he had wanted to go directly through town. He immediately began screaming in a fit of uncontrolled anger. I stared at my hands in my lap, looking up once to see the man in the car next to us staring as George ranted and raved. I quickly looked down again, too afraid to cry.

"Stupid, that was so stupid. Now we're going miles out of our way. I'm going to pull over and put you out, you hear me? Get out, get out, stupid!"

I glanced to the side of the road to see how much room was there in case he put me out. He kept driving and finally stopped yelling and I relaxed a bit. Then I began to fantasize about what I would do if he really forced me out of the car. I never had cash on me, nor did I have my own credit card. There were no cell phones back then. I decided

I'd get off the road, look for a police cruiser or a store. Otherwise I'd have to just knock on someone's door and ask them to call the police for me. George's mom would get me a bus ticket back to Cleveland. Getting the police involved would mean I would have proof of what he was like. And he couldn't blame it on me this time.

There were times his anger affected others and I suffered the repercussions. The couple upstairs walked heavily. George would often take the broom handle and hit the ceiling. He hit the ceiling one too many times and one morning, after he left for class, they jumped up and down and played their electric organ so loudly our windows shook. I held my hands over my ears until it stopped and then went right to the Dean's office, begging him to let us move to an upstairs unit, even though it was against all the rules. I said George had a concentration problem and couldn't study with the noise up above, so he finally allowed us to move.

We graduated from Lee in August of 1982 and George enrolled in the Church of God School of Theology (now Pentecostal Theological Seminary), where I got hired as the receptionist. We were able to stay in our apartment. George attended there for a semester or two and we made good friends with two other couples, Warren and Lois and Leo and Kathi. I coveted the times we spent with these friends because being around them gave me a reprieve.

Cooking dinner at Kathi's house in 1983

George's anger caused a few issues for me at work. As receptionist, I handled all the calls coming in to the seminary and greeted all visitors. One day a visiting minister came in just as George was yelling at me on the phone. The minister noticed I was not real cheerful, as I was trying to keep from crying. He complained to the president that I was not friendly and I got chided. George often called and screamed with some imaginary problem and I would have to deal with him and perform my job duties. One day George had me so upset a male professor relieved me so I could compose myself. When George called back to yell at me again, he informed George I was upset and had to take a break.

Now that George knew it was obvious to the staff that he mistreated me, he felt he had to do something to redeem himself. One day I went to lunch with some secretaries and when I came back, people were grinning knowingly. I walked in and saw a huge flower arrangement on my desk. Everyone waited as I looked at the card, and then I saw George peeking around the door of the auditorium adjacent to my desk. I asked, "Are these from *you*?" Then I started crying because he had done something nice for me. Unfortunately, a wife always knows when she's given guilt flowers.

Dissatisfied with the programs offered at our church's seminary in Cleveland, Tennessee, George applied to a seminary in Ohio. We spent the summer of 1983 in Fort Lauderdale, living with his mom and working to pay off our loans. It was one of the few times George worked during our marriage. Then George turned his sights toward Ashland Theological Seminary in Ashland, Ohio, where he was accepted for the fall term of 1984.

Chapter 5

Ashland Theological Seminary

*G*eorge transferred to Ashland Theological Seminary (ATS) in the fall of 1984, traveling on ahead to find an apartment. I used this opportunity to try to leave, telling him on the phone that I was tired of his abuse. I loved my job and I knew his mother would allow me to stay with her. She had seen how George treated me and offered me emotional and financial support. One of her favorite comments was, "He is one hundred percent wrong."

Unfortunately, George said he would come back home if I didn't join him. That would mean I would have to find a place to live. My salary was just above minimum wage and apartments were not cheap in Fort Lauderdale. He also promised, if I joined him, he would go to counseling for his anger, something he had never agreed to in the past. Reluctantly, I boarded a plane to Cleveland, Ohio in the midst of a tropical depression.

When George picked me up at the Cleveland airport he hugged me, but I just felt numb. Looking over his shoulder everything looked blurry through my unshed tears. I was obviously not as happy to see him as he was to see me.

We moved into a first floor unit in seminary housing and I was hired at Ashland University as the Library Director's secretary. I reminded George of his promise to get counseling, so he made an appointment. Things were looking up. If George really changed, maybe I could someday have the baby I wanted so desperately. After a couple of counseling sessions, however, George's therapist had to stop due to cancer treatments. Making matters worse, I became aware that, in the short time before I arrived, George had become infatuated with a female student.

Before I married, I had dreamed of my man being my knight in shining armor, a strong Christian man of moral character with whom I would feel safe. I envisioned a man who would be a spiritual giant, taking the lead in family worship and in our household. He would cherish me in every way and always be kind and patient. George's first act of abuse caused him to slip a bit off the saddle of his white horse. Every day he slipped a little more.

When I joined him in Ashland I learned he had other traits that caused him to finally fall off the saddle completely, denting his shiny armor, his white horse galloping off into the distance. While it had been devastating discovering my white knight was mean to me, I really didn't think he could cause me to sink any lower. Then he defeminized me by flirting with someone else, pushing my female identity into the ground and making me feel completely worthless.

Laura

I had noticed, soon after we married, that George's behavior around other women was different from other married male students. There was no shortage of beautiful young women on campus, but most guys would give a casual glance and that was all. George would lock his eyes on to a woman until she finally noticed him, giving the impression he had either a wounded male ego or an over-inflated one. I had always wondered how far he would go and if he would become easily distracted.

Laura was a gorgeous former model who had a husband back home, but apparently was not too happy in her marriage. She had a constant entourage of male admirers. It was hard not to like her, even though my husband obviously liked her too much. While I understood the attraction, I didn't expect George to join the group that followed her around. At least the other guys flocking to her were single.

One night at a party I realized everyone else had noticed George's behavior as well. When she left the room and he followed her, everyone grew silent and looked at me with pity in their eyes. One Friday evening we attended another gathering. I was exhausted from a full week of classes and my full time job. George was sitting on the floor beside me when Laura came up behind him and started giving him a neck massage. I glanced over and noticed he had an erection and, feeling humiliated, lay down with my head on his leg so no one would see. Soon Brian, another male student, suggested George take me home because I was tired. When we got home he was extremely angry because he had to leave and I knew it was because he wanted to be around Laura. For once I didn't care and went to bed, saddened that he chose Laura over me.

George brought Laura home for lunch one day and, as I prepared lunch for the three of us, they stood close together at the living room window, murmuring. I doubted Laura would really be attracted to George and assumed she was sharing some concern with him, hoping he would pray with her. After lunch they left for class, but a few minutes later I heard a knock on the door. It was Laura. She had skipped the class they had together so that she could visit with me. She asked if she could style my hair. Soon she had my hair puffy and more make up on my face than I ever wore. I sensed she was trying to help me in her own way. She said something about George and guys like him being so easy to read and then left before George could return from class. I quickly combed out my hair and washed my face, knowing George would be suspicious to see me looking like that. When George came home he was furious. "That bitch!" he yelled. Then he told me that Laura had told him she really didn't like him much and that if she had to choose between having him or me for a friend, she would choose me. I secretly chuckled, knowing someone must have said something to Laura about his inappropriate behavior.

I gathered that most men longed for beauty and that having a gorgeous woman gave them some feeling of achievement over other men, and that they liked being admired. On the other hand, I knew countless men who were committed to, and honored, their wives. There was even a *single* male student who was different. I watched him when Laura was around and he paid her no mind at all. One evening he came by when George was in an evening class. Having recently recovered some journals that I had no access to for years, I found where I'd written his comments down verbatim:

"People know what's going on. George looks foolish following her around and he *is* a fool. Girls like her are only so much fluff, just wanting men to notice them. You're pretty inside and out and lots of guys would give their right arm to have a wife like you. I'd snatch you up in a second if you were single. If he's not careful, God will take you away and give you to somebody who will appreciate the gift He's given."

While Brian's words were comforting, I doubted I was as valuable as he said. His words were just words, and I lived with the reality of how I was treated every day. If I was all that good, then why did my own husband seek Laura's attention? Why wasn't I enough for him?

George had lost my love and now he had lost my trust. At Lee, our ethics professor had insisted that flirting with someone else while married, even without words, was a relationship, a promise of something more, a sharing of intimacy, and definitely emotional cheating. By seeking Laura's attention, he had made me feel less than a woman. It had sealed the fate of our marriage because I no longer cared about making it work and had no feelings left for him. The memory of his flirting replayed in my mind and any love I had left for him died. While I had held hope with each occurrence of abuse, I no longer even cared about having hope.

Seeing my husband as less than I thought he was should have been a positive thing. But his actions of flirting had a further negative consequence. My self-esteem plummeted even more. I doubted I had what it took to make it on my own and I became extremely hopeless. It would be a long time before I understood it was his loss, and that I had a lot of value as a woman and a life partner.

I found myself lying in bed at night crying for someone else, a fantasy love who would be my soul mate. My fantasies were not just sexual. I was dying for affection of another kind as well. I wanted to be held and cherished, valued and protected. I wanted that knight in shining armor I had dreamed of as a child, when I planted the magical seeds in the little bridge behind our house. I wanted someone who would love me so much he would never want another. I did allow my mind to wander toward the physical, wondering how it would feel to have someone really make love to me, setting me free. Was such a thing even possible? I would have to really feel safe to ever feel free like that with a man.

In the future, when I mentioned Laura, George insisted she had meant nothing. But everything we do in life is a choice and every choice we make means something. Love is not a feeling; it's a commitment, a decision every day to choose your spouse. I still believe he would have gone with her in a second if she'd been willing. He saw her, and he chose her over his wife.

The Beagle

Walking to work one day I looked down and saw a beagle walking beside me. He was regal and gentle. When I reached to pat his head, he looked up at me and my finger hit his eye. He didn't flinch, but kept his head steady, allowing me to pet him some more. My heart was stolen by those big brown eyes and I longed for a dog of my own. Not just any dog. I wanted a beagle. He walked me right up to the library door and then took off across campus. When I told George about it, his only comment was he'd never want a dog in the house.

10/20/87

I was making dinner while George fiddled at the table with his potted plants. Suddenly I heard an exasperated sigh, a bang and then stomping. My stomach knotted up as I looked to see what was happening. He had grown impatient while trimming a plant, dumping it on the floor and stomping the dirt into the carpet. "A little help," he yelled, "is that too much to ask for? I just needed a little help."

I felt so much disgust the words escaped before I had time to think. "I'm making your dinner. Why didn't you ask?"

He rushed over to me and raised his fist. Realizing I shouldn't have said anything, I backed up a step. His fist opened, he pointed his finger and I knew what was coming. He started poking at me so I arched my back over the counter, but couldn't get far enough away. His steely finger was poking my chest over and over. He kept poking until my eyes got teary and then walked away, mumbling, "Clean that up." And I did, quickly, so dinner wouldn't be late.

I regretted losing a nice plant. If George had left it alone, I would have tended to it. Now it was in the trash. He always had to take over things, even rearranging my kitchen cabinets. I tried to think of one thing I had that was mine alone, that he didn't try to take away from me.

That night dad called to inform me my stepmother's aunt had shot herself. After hanging up I sat on the floor and wept silently, whispering a prayer for her soul and the family. I hadn't heard George walk up beside me.

"What's wrong?" he asked irritably.

"My aunt shot herself."

"Cry for me!" he yelled, beating his hand against his chest. "I'm going to kill myself too, so cry for me."

His words somehow caused my emotions of sadness to dissipate like a vapor. I marveled at how often I would seem to lose my feelings when George lost control. I wondered where the emotions went to. Did they retreat somewhere deep inside me? Would they fester there like a disease, making me sick inside? I had not heard of dissociation or numbing. I just felt frustrated that I could never think of a successful reply, freezing up like a zombie when he yelled. It wouldn't have done any good no matter what I said anyhow, because he had a way of twisting around anything I tried to say. He seemed to live in a whole different reality.

If I'd expected a sympathetic word, I was disappointed and amazed at his selfishness. I didn't put two and two together at that time, but I think the familiarity of the paramount man in my life threatening suicide pushed a panic button in me. Why did the men in my life want to die? Even Kenny had wished he was dead at times! As I walked to the bedroom to study, I also found myself wondering why I should care if George killed himself.

I had stopped crying in front of George, stubbornly refusing to allow him to see how much he scared me. I still cried, but only in private.

December 1, 1987, Journal

> *I wish my self-esteem mattered to him as much as his matters to me. Even with how he's treated me and how I no longer love him, I could never treat him how he treats me. I awoke with a headache and stumbled in to the kitchen to make breakfast. Dropping a heavy measuring cup, it hit the corner of the counter, glass flying everywhere. George had set out his vitamins and protein powder and, fearing they were full of glass, he took his arm and brushed them all into the*

floor. "What a waste!" he shouted. "You know how expensive these things are, right?" I felt badly enough about the accident; his anger made me feel even worse. Why were things more important than me? I again realized I'd never let myself get pregnant with him. His anger would devastate a child's self-esteem. Children break and spill things and make messes. I had wanted children so badly, but I knew I had to sacrifice them while with him. Hopefully I could get away while I was still young enough to start a family.

Christmas 1987

I've always loved Christmas lights. There wasn't money, however, for decorations and I knew better than to ask. Our friends had two trees and extra decorations so they shared with us. After I decorated the tree, I stood back and admired how realistic and festive it was.

Warren and Lois had sent us bus tickets to come and spend Christmas with them in Wilson, NC where he was pastoring. The day we were to leave, I got up to make breakfast before going to work. The bus was leaving that night and George wanted the tree down before we left. He started un-trimming it while I cooked.

I soon heard the familiar sounds of frustration from the living room and peeked around to see him impatiently tugging at the light strings. I knew better than to intervene or offer help, instead returning to my biscuit batter. Soon I heard stomping and peeked around to find him stomping on my beautiful tree. When I sat our food on the table I realized my six foot tree had been reduced to fit into a kitchen trash bag. I choked down breakfast, but couldn't hide my tears this time. "Cry for me!" he shouted, red faced, "Cry for me, not the tree, cry for me!"

When George went to the bathroom I rushed into the living room and rescued some cookie tins I'd had under the tree, hiding them quickly under the bed. Then I washed dishes and prepared to leave for work. I walked to the bathroom and told him I was leaving.

"Wait a minute," he ordered. He came out and walked into the living room. Picking up the trash bag with my tree, decorations and lights in it, he shoved it at me. "Throw this in the dumpster on your way out."

I took it from him silently and walked out the back door of our building. He couldn't see me now so I let the tears freely fall, not even caring if anyone saw me. As I dumped my tree into the dumpster I found myself hating him.

My boots had holes in them and by the time I walked the seven blocks to work the snow had come through and soaked my socks. I normally packed spare shoes and socks, but in the commotion I had forgotten. Later I felt heaviness in my chest and had chills. I recognized the onset of bronchitis and wondered how it hit me so quickly. I hadn't felt ill when I left the apartment a few hours earlier. I wondered if the shock of George's destructive anger could have caused my body to sicken.

I stayed at work all day, not wanting to go home with him there. On the way home I went by the student clinic and was given some antibiotics and cough medicine. I dreaded the long trip ahead that night, on a bus with people smoking. When I got home from work I said, "I'm sick, I'm lying down until dinner time," and walked into the bedroom. He didn't even ask what was wrong.

Africa, summer, 1988

Walking down the hallway of the seminary during the spring semester, I noticed a flyer on the wall about an opportunity to teach in Africa for the summer. I thought it might be of interest to George, since his goal was to be a professor. Some teaching experience might help bolster his self-confidence so he could finally find a career and help support us. I should have known it would be a bad idea to be stuck abroad with him. He applied and was accepted for the mission experience. We took out another student loan to cover the cost. I resigned my job, knowing we'd have to tough out our final year without my salary once we got back home.

We flew to New York on a cloudy, stormy day, and then boarded an evening flight to London on the biggest plane I'd ever seen. In London we boarded a South African jumbo jet for Johannesburg, called Jo-burg by the natives. Our last flight was a small prop job that took us the short distance to Bulawayo, Zimbabwe. The airport at Bulawayo was tiny and we were carefully scrutinized by soldiers armed with shotguns. They almost impounded George's store of vitamins and supplements until he showed them the receipts. I was holding my breath, knowing he'd really be in a bad humor if he had to throw out hundreds of dollars' worth of supplements. The missionary couple we would be interning under picked us up and took us to an upstairs room in what used to be a YMCA, which now housed the Theological College of Zimbabwe.

We awoke that night to the sound of clicking in the room. George tiptoed to the light switch and we discovered the floor covered with small, strange insects that came in through the open window near the ceiling. It wouldn't be our only struggle with bugs. My worst memory of Africa involved ants. They were everywhere and George reacted typically. "Get rid of them or I'll go home and leave you here!"

I was so frightened of being abandoned in Africa I went to the principal and begged for some ant repellent. I even confessed that George had an anger problem. He didn't seem to take the anger thing seriously, but he did give me some ant powder.

George seemed to always be hungry and I often left food on my plate for him to finish. Our diet consisted mostly of *sadsa*, an African staple kind of like grits, bean soup and a fatty looking meat we dubbed "mystery meat." That afternoon I sat on the porch to eat my dinner. When I looked down at my plate, I saw a black speck in my *sadsa*. When I realized it was an ant it was the last straw. Nobody was around and I let loose and cried my heart out.

After dinner I went up to our room and washed my face. When I took out my metal comb to comb my hair, I saw something that hadn't been there before, my name scratched in to the handle, with a cross behind it. I know it was just scratches, but to me it was a moment of grace that often seemed to come when I felt at the end of my own strength.

The last part of our mission experience was spent in Pietermaritzburg, South Africa at the Evangelical Bible College of South Africa or EBSemSA. Our time there was a bit better. I was not given a class to teach because the principal felt my task was to support George in his ministry. Food storage was limited so I would walk to the market each day to buy fresh food for dinner.

Since my major at seminary was Church History and Judaic Studies with an emphasis on Holocaust studies, I was asked to address the whole school on the importance of Holocaust remembrance. I was petrified in front of everyone, but mostly knowing the critiquing eyes of my husband were upon me. Sure enough, he pointed out all of my mistakes when we got home.

Sitting at World View near Bulawayo; posing in my new sari in Pietermaritzburg; standing with Bobbies in London on Downing Street.

We were able to spend a few days in London at the home of a co-missionary before we returned to Ashland in August. Back in the States, it felt strange to walk in to supermarkets and see all the choices offered there. Even handling U.S. currency seemed strange. I had a renewed appreciation for our country.

Now we had the task of figuring out how to live the next school year with no income. We'd had our phone disconnected and our broken-down car hauled away before we left for Africa. My advisor asked me to be his teaching assistant my senior year, allowing me to take my classes tuition free rather than half price, which would help. It wasn't enough, however, to quell my fear. It had been years since I hadn't earned a regular income. I had worked since I was fourteen, never wanting to depend on anyone else. It had even embarrassed me all the times George had asked his mother for money.

A friend offered to take me grocery shopping with her once a week. I had a strict budget and would tally the items before putting them in my cart. One day the cashier added up my purchases and I was mortified to see I had miscalculated. As I picked out a few items from my bags to be subtracted, I heard exasperated sighs behind me.

When I got home some friends from church were visiting. Their little girl was looking around and then came and stood by me. "Where is your phone?" she asked. I told her we didn't have one. "Where is your sofa?" Again I told her we didn't have one, only two chairs. She had already heard us telling our friends we'd had our car towed away. "Wow, you guys are really poor!" she said, making us all chuckle. But behind my chuckle was a deep-set fear.

In Africa I had often stopped eating before I felt full, pushing some of my food to George. Again I tried cutting back on my portions, this time to save money. I was finding comfort in controlling what I put in my body, and how my figure was responding. I normally made us pudding cake cups for dessert one night a week. The next dessert night, after eating, I went into the bathroom and made myself throw up. I felt so embarrassed and ashamed over our poverty and powerless and afraid without my job. I wanted to rid myself of the shame that seemed to cling to me. And I needed to feel in control of something in life. And so I began to control how much I ate and how much food I allowed staying in my body. The skinnier I got the more attractive I felt. I always knew what I was doing and why I was doing it, and when I decided it had gone on long enough I stopped. But for a brief time it served a purpose.

<u>Spring 1989</u>

Dad and my stepmom were coming to visit. I felt a tug in my stomach, realizing it wasn't a good time for company and wondering how George would act. And where would they sleep? We had two bedrooms, but one was George's office/gym. I borrowed an air mattress for us to sleep on in his office, and they could have our bed.

What would I feed them? In my family it's traditional that you cook for company, rather than going out to eat. Besides we couldn't afford to go out, and it would be rude to allow company to buy our meals. I planned a meager meal with what we had.

When they arrived I sensed George's discomfort and suggested he join a softball game that was in progress. I knew it offended my parents when he left, and tried to smooth it over. My stepmom started telling me what a nice time they'd had at Kenny's before coming to see us. Kenny and his wife had spent a lot of time showing them around and had taken them out to nice restaurants. Apologizing, I told them that finals were starting and George was under pressure. They weren't convinced so I finally opened up and told them my secret. When I saw the look of sadness and defeat on my dad's face, I felt an overwhelming anxiety that I couldn't understand; a mixture of guilt, shame, grief, sadness and fear. Rather than accepting any comfort, I found myself trying to comfort him.

We got through dinner and they decided to find a hotel room and leave the next morning. I went to visit them later at their room, promising I would try to get free of George. When I got home, George was in the hallway talking to our neighbor. I was so distraught I did the unthinkable. Right in front of our neighbor, I blurted out to George, "You *could* have made them feel more welcome." Then I fled into our bedroom, where he followed a second later. He sat on the bed beside me, telling me I'd embarrassed him. As he spoke I tried to open my bottom dresser drawer and it stuck. Suddenly it came loose, hitting his leg. He knew it was an accident, but he stood up and started pounding my purse with his fists, over and over. It was beside me on the bed and I could hear crunching noises. "He'd rather be pounding me," I remember thinking.

George grabbed some books and left while I examined my purse, finding many objects inside broken. I wondered why he always broke my things instead of his. Not knowing where he was made me nervous, so I went looking and found him in the library. I pretended to be sorry to calm him down.

I wondered why, for months to come, I could not get my dad's sad face out of my mind and why I felt some urgent need to make sure he was alright. His face would invade my mind and dreams, causing me an overwhelming sense of anxiety about his well-being.

April 1989: An Ordinary Day

It's time to go home from my teaching assistant job and, like every day around this time, I have butterflies. I know he took a test today in

New Testament Greek. I hope he did well. God, please, let him have done well. If he did well he might be okay tonight. If he didn't, well, I'll have to pay.

I climb the steps and my heart is racing. I open the door. Where is he? He's not at the table studying. I hear the familiar clink of weights hitting each other. Oh he's working out. That's good. He loves working out. I don't call out a greeting because he hates being interrupted.

I hear a "hi Littles" from the back bedroom and answer "hi" with relief. When he calls me "Littles" it means he's in a good mood. Glancing at the menu, I prepare to start dinner. Spaghetti tonight. An easy meal.

Suddenly he's in the kitchen, behind me. He gives me a quick peck on the cheek. Before I can ask about his test, he looks at the noodles I have on the counter and he starts in.

"I thought we were having beans tonight. Tonight is Tuesday, veggie night."

I feel flushed and dizzy, grabbing the counter so I don't fall. "Veggie night is tomorrow night."

"Don't you remember I changed it?" He hits the wall. "Nobody listens to me. Why do I even bother talking to you? You never listen."

"But it's not on the schedule."

"Do I have to do everything? You should have changed the schedule as soon as I told you to."

"I'm sorry," I stammer. "I forgot. I didn't soak the beans so can we start the new schedule next week? I won't forget next week."

*"We have no choice now, do we?" He walks over and starts poking my chest. "Why doesn't anyone ever listen to me? I'm just talking to myself. I move my mouth but nobody hears. It's just **an exercise in***

futility." *He stops poking me and starts hitting himself in the head with his hands. "Aaaaaaaahhhhhggggg!" He knocks the pan off the counter on his way out of the kitchen, but thankfully I have not filled it with water yet.*

I shakily pick up the pot and fill it with water. Hearing the shower run, I know I have a few minutes of reprieve.

After his shower he walks in like nothing happened, sniffing the sauce and glancing at the clock to see if I'm going to make the 6:00 deadline. I glance at it too and let out a thankful sigh. I'll make it. He walks over to me and pecks me on the cheek again. "Smells good. Hey Littles, would you mind Xeroxing some papers for me tomorrow?"

At dinner we rarely talk, but tonight he has a strange request. "Anna, how do you read? I feel like I have to underline every sentence, or highlight every important word and it takes forever. I wish somebody could help me read. If I just knew how to read properly then it would be easier. I read the same paragraph ten times and I still don't get it. There has to be a proper way to read. If only I could find a book about how to read. Could you look in the library at work tomorrow and see if there's something like that, a book on how to read? Then I could read the book on how to read and it would help me know what the right method for reading is. I just need some help." His voice is getting louder again. "I just need somebody to help me. Why can't somebody just help me?"

Forcing a mouthful of noodles down, I promise him I'll look for a book tomorrow.

While he's brushing his teeth, I wash as many dishes as I can. I fill one side of the sink with rinse water, so I don't have to run any water when he sits down in the living room. Once the television goes on I'll have to be quiet. I'm almost finished when it goes on. I accidentally hit a dish against the edge of the sink and freeze.

"Anna, are you almost finished? I can't hear the TV. Do you have to make so much noise?"

I finish the dishes and wipe my hands, wondering how to manage a week of meals with the food I bought. I'd better go check the food pantry to see if anyone has made donations. When a commercial comes on I tell him where I'm going. I take a couple of empty bags and head out, hoping no one is in the pool room outside the pantry. It's embarrassing when someone sees me take food because it's there for poor students.

No one is around as I open the door to the pantry with a hopeful heart. I moan with gratitude when I see how well stocked it is. I quickly stuff my bags, hoping no one will see me walk back to our apartment. What a treasure! There are paper towels, toilet paper, dish detergent, spaghetti sauce, noodles and tuna canned in water.

George sees me walk in. Without thinking I blurt out, "Look what I found in the pantry." I show him my treasures and as he comments my heart falls. "Good, now you won't need a whole forty dollars for groceries next week."

"Yes," I agree. "I probably won't."

Food is a big issue to George. Everything has to be name brands. Sometimes I save bottles of name brand items and pour other items into them so he won't know. It's the only way I can afford to feed us and keep him calm. Then I take the off brand cans and bottles out to the dumpster when he's not looking. Borrowing a quote from the Bible I often catch myself thinking the dumpster "hides a multitude of sins."

As I shower I'm hoping he won't want sex tonight. I know if he does, he'll go right to the bathroom when he's done. He'll wash out his mouth, spitting over and over. Then he'll wash his penis and then scrub his hands. Sometimes he just asks me to service him, which is fine with me. He reminds me to have a tissue handy to spit in and to make sure I wash out my mouth. And then he runs the water a long time while he washes his penis free of my saliva.

As I fall asleep I wonder if it's like this for everyone. I imagine how I wish it would be with someone who loves my body: He'll kiss me and stroke my body with his hands. His hands will feel warm and I'll feel the love in his touch. Everywhere he touches me will burn with a wonderful sensation. He will enjoy touching me and will not think it's dirty. He will touch my cheeks and gaze into my eyes and tell me how precious I am to him. I'll reach up with my right hand and brush his hair back and tenderly cup his face in my hands. He will be happy with me. And then he will hold me while we go to sleep. If I breathe on him he'll like it. I'll lay my head on his chest and feel his heartbeat. He'll hold me all night long.

I fall asleep, feeling incredibly lonely. And so ends an ordinary day.

May 1989

As we approached the end of our seminary education, George's motivation to work on his thesis waned and his silences would go on for days. I walked softly, waiting for the explosion to happen. If George didn't finish his thesis, the last five years would have been in vain, and he still wouldn't have a career.

When I went to my teaching assistant job, my advisor, Dr. Reiss, took one look at my face and asked me what was wrong. I explained

I was fearful George was giving up on his thesis. I started crying and he pulled me in to his arms. It felt odd to have a man holding me in comfort, but it was a nice change.

That night Dr. Reiss came by our apartment and spoke to George. I brewed Dr. Reiss a pot of his beloved coffee and he spent at least an hour trying to encourage George. I was appreciative of his efforts and felt more hopeful when he left. I was able to sleep all night for the first time in weeks.

Unfortunately, George still couldn't seem to tackle the last part of his thesis. I was sitting in my Old Testament Theology class in the front row when I began to cry silently. *I sure seemed to cry a lot!*

When class let out my professor approached me before I could escape, asking me what was troubling me. When I told him George had stopped working on his thesis, he said he'd see what he could do. True to his word, he spoke up at the next staff meeting, getting George an extension on his thesis. George could go through the graduation ceremony, receiving an empty diploma holder until he finished his thesis. And we could stay in our apartment while he finished.

As graduation got closer I began to wonder what we would do next. One night I got on my knees. "Oh God," I begged, "Will you please get me out of this? Please show me how. Please teach me what's wrong with me, why I freeze when he yells. Teach me how to trust You and have enough faith to earn Your help. Make me strong enough to leave before I get too old to find a good husband who will love me and let me have children. Please God, forgive me if I've done wrong, and hear my prayer." As an afterthought, I added, "And a beagle please." I am somewhat of a mystic and I believe sometimes God offers comfort in small and sometimes unusual ways. When I shut my mouth and listened for God I thought of the number two.

My heart soared with hope. Maybe God was telling me I'd be free in two years. I could handle that.

It would take much longer than two years to finally escape. But on my birthday in February of 2002 the man of my dreams would buy me a beagle. His birthdate would be 02/22/02. That little fur ball would be my "child" and he would also be my little angel from God. And when I finally married the man of my dreams, it would be in the month of February, the month of my birth.

August 1989

George's mom flew up for our graduation. She had won 500 dollars at Bingo which she gave us for a graduation gift, 250 dollars each. I automatically handed my share to George. We went through our ceremony, everyone standing and clapping for me when they announced *summa cum laude*. I smiled but I was thinking, "With how stupid I am, my coursework must have been easy," and I was hoping George wouldn't be jealous.

My New Testament Theology professor chose my final research paper to keep on file in the library as a go-by for new students. He also surprised me by asking that I consider being his student teacher the next year, a paid position. It was an amazing honor and could have changed the course of my life. I never told George of his offer and I declined, naturally. George was the one who wanted to teach. If he knew that *his advisor* had offered me a teaching position, it would have had terrible consequences for me. Besides I really doubted I could handle the job and secretly felt the professor saw more talent in me than I really possessed.

The Insanity of Indecision

George finished his thesis and received his diploma and we knew we had to make plans to vacate our apartment. He contacted Warren and Lois and they invited us to come to their house and stay until they could help us find our own place and jobs. When we got there Warren helped George unpack our U-Haul trailer into storage and showed us around. He found a job for George delivering milk, if George would accept it. That would never do. George whispered angrily to me that he had expected Warren to find him a ministry position. I begged him to take the job and give it time. But he told me we were leaving. Warren helped George pack up again and we left for Fort Lauderdale.

George's mother's house was stifling hot when we arrived. Not only was the air conditioner broken, but George's grandmother was living there. Not a pleasant woman, she had been a cruel mother to George's mom, and had been mean to George when he was a child. I could tell George was depressed and withdrawn and very unhappy to be there. He decided we'd been better off back in North Carolina and chose to give it another try. Warren and Lois agreed that we could come back and we set out again. We hadn't even unpacked our trailer.

Back in North Carolina, Warren once again helped George unpack our possessions into a storage locker and helped us look for yet another apartment. For the second time, we put down a deposit on a place, and for the second time, we lost it as George again decided not to stay. Again we headed back to Fort Lauderdale.

Eventually, Warren sent George a letter of reprimand for how he treated me and for not being a good husband or steward. Although he wrote it in a loving, supportive way, George was angry and insisted Warren was no longer his friend. During our back and forth foray,

Warren had observed George's bizarre behavior at last and was witness to his anger and abuse. Once again, my secret was out and I feared that more friends were alienated.

George's mom had the air conditioner repaired, but she stayed in her room most of the time watching television and George's grandmother would sit in a rocking chair in the living room where we were.

"She's watching me," George complained to his mom. "She's always watching me."

Finally his mom had grandma come into her bedroom to watch television with her.

When George's mom went to Bingo one night, George got angry and picked his grandma up out of her rocker, carried her into her bedroom and sat her down, ordering her to stay there. I followed him, terrified he was going to hurt her. When he sat her down, she stumbled and fell. I watched to make sure she was okay, knowing I couldn't keep silent. That night I slipped into his mom's room, telling her what George had done. She waited until the next day and told George that grandma had told her, so he wouldn't punish me. Then she ordered him to never touch her again. His mom soon placed her mother in a nursing home, but George's attitude toward his mom was forever changed. She had embarrassed him and had taken grandma's side over his. She was now the enemy!

George was too much a coward to say anything to his mom's face, but he began to make comments under his breath whenever she walked through the room he was in. I told her everything he said about her. He thought I was on his side because the alternative was unthinkable to him. But his mom and I both despised his hostile behavior. Soon his comments were loud enough for his mom to hear as he called her "jerk" when she walked through the room. She pretended not to hear him.

I forget what happened, but one day after grandma was gone George got angry with me and picked me up and carried me into our bedroom. Closing the door, he ordered me to stay there. He could bully his grandmother that way, but not me. I opened the door and followed him to the living room and sat down beside him. I think I felt bolder because I was no longer all alone with him. I knew if he started pounding me physically his mom would intervene.

"You'd better start looking for a job because I'm leaving," I told him.

If I'd had a cell phone back then, I'm pretty sure I would have phoned 911 from the bedroom and told the cops my husband had imprisoned me in our bedroom. It turned out I was way too much of a coward then to follow up on my threats. But he never carried me into the bedroom or shut me up in a room again.

Chapter 6

Fort Lauderdale P.D.

I worked as a substitute teacher for a while, earning a little income. But I knew I needed to find a full-time job. I soon found a position at a large church in Fort Lauderdale as the senior pastor's secretary. George's mom generously drove me back and forth to work each day. Most mornings she would take me to breakfast and these times with her, away from George, became my favorite times. George's mom commented some mornings that men noticed me, but their greetings of "good morning" were, in my mind, just polite gestures, as I couldn't imagine a man being really attracted to me.

In front of George's mom's house in Ft. Lauderdale.

I did not like my job. The pastor was unkind to his employees, and he ran the church, in his words, "like a business." I couldn't quit until I had another job to go to. George did not look for a job, fearing he would get "stuck", and tried instead to find ways to draw attention to himself so that he might be wanted for some type of ministry. His first venture was to spend a week on the streets to draw attention to the homeless. His second was to join a group called "Volunteers for Israel" during Operation Desert Storm. We had been saving for a car, but he used that money to fund the trip to Israel, where he would work in nursing homes or wherever needed.

In 1992 George studied and became certified as an EMT. He was unemployed until March 1994 when he attended the Broward Fire Academy and became certified as a firefighter. Again he did not find a full-time job, but was a volunteer at the Plantation Fire Department where he received $5.00 per call when he felt like monitoring his radio and responding to fire calls.

I applied to the City of Ft. Lauderdale in May of 1992 and was hired to work in the Police Department starting on June 24, 1992 as a Clerk Typist. I happily resigned my job of three years at the church. One of the co-pastors warned me that a police department was not a good atmosphere for a Christian girl and that I would be working around rough men who cursed and treated women badly. Ironically, I was treated a lot better at the P.D. than I had been at the large church.

I was assigned to the Fraud Unit where most of the detectives were committed to their families and to getting bad guys off the streets. Many of them were church goers as well. I had the best boss ever and made friends with the other secretaries. Work became my haven. George had often quoted Scarecrow from the Wizard of Oz, saying, "If she only had a brain," but my boss gave me responsibilities and opportunities to use my own creativity and decision-making skills. The guys at work didn't think I was stupid and never criticized me, and they laughed at my jokes. If George had ever walked in to my squad by surprise, he would not have recognized me. He'd have wondered why I looked happy and self-confident and how I could do anything on my own, without him telling me how. He would have thought, "This isn't right; she can't do this, not without me. I have to be here to tell her what to do and how to do it." I felt smart, needed and a valuable asset to the squad and began to break out of my shell.

A Trip to the Mall, 1993

I dreaded weekends at home. One Saturday morning George couldn't finish his run, which always signaled the start of a bad day. We got home from the track and he started in. "I'm losing strength and muscle tone. Look at my legs." (as his hands circled around his skinny thigh). "If you'd help me with my diet, I could gain some muscle. I need more protein. Why do I even talk to you? You don't listen and you don't care and you don't help me. I'm totally alone in this and it doesn't matter to anyone but me."

He had poked at my face; his iron hard finger just inches away. I knew it would feel like a bee sting if his finger hit my face, so I pushed his arm away and said "stop" and walked toward the bed-room. Following me, he came around the bed, trapping me in the corner. I berated myself for being so foolish. He started smacking both sides of his head with his hands, and I took the opportunity to quickly duck around him. Heading for the kitchen, I looked back to see he'd gone in the bathroom. I busied myself wiping the counter until I heard the toilet flush, then braced for his entrance. Suddenly,

I heard him singing in the bathroom. "He really is crazy," I thought. "It's just not normal to go from irate to calm in seconds."

He walked in to the kitchen and, as if nothing had happened, asked, "You feel like going to the mall? I could use some new shoes." I know my voice was shaky, but I said okay, and told him I'd get ready, already fearing the unpredictability of the experience ahead. I could never control all the circumstances we might confront that would set him off in a heartbeat, so I always dreaded going anywhere with him.

Entering the mall, we approached the shoe store. As he perused the window display, he played that game with my hand in his. He'd squeeze my hand once, and I knew I was supposed to squeeze back once. Then he'd squeeze twice and then three times in a pattern, waiting for me to repeat the pattern with my hand. I glanced sideways at him and smiled, hoping he would think I was having a nice time. I commented, "It looks like they have the color you want, now if they only have your size," but I was thinking about the words to a song about how "I can't be myself when I'm with you."

We walked in like a happy couple and thankfully a clerk was free. Checking out later, I thought "mission successful" and looked forward to getting home. I was so giddy with relief that I began to share something that happened at work that day. Major mistake! I could sense he was feeling jealous. "At least you have people to talk to during the day. I'm always alone and I don't have anyone to talk to."

"Idiot," I scolded myself. "You know not to let him suspect you have fun at work. Make him think you hate it and that you're miserable like he is. Misery loves company."

I was thankful we could go home now, and breathed a bit easier as we walked toward the mall exit. Home wasn't safe, but it was predictable and I could walk in to other rooms or in to the bathroom or

I could get busy making lunch. Lunch! Oh God, no! It's lunch time. My stomach clenched so hard I almost doubled over. He looked at me. "What's wrong, Anna? You're holding your stomach. Are you hungry? It *is* lunch time."

"No, no, no, no, no, please don't say it. Please, God, don't let him ask."

As if on cue he spoke those forbidden words: "Where do you want to eat?"

The mall started spinning. My heart started racing so hard I thought I would die. No, no, no! Eating out always went the same and today would be no different.

He'll ask me where I want to eat and if I don't choose, he'll be angry and if I do choose and it's the wrong thing, he'll be angry. He might go along with a choice I don't even care about (because I really don't care where we eat or what we eat). I just want him to pick a damn place and we'll eat. It's just food to me. If he makes me choose and he doesn't like it, then he doesn't have to be responsible for the bad decision. When I eat with him the food is tasteless anyhow. To him it's a major life choice and what he puts in his mouth is of major import. And if I choose the wrong thing and he goes along with it, he'll eat angrily (yes one can eat angrily) and I'll wonder if the people around us can tell. And I'll have to try to make conversation. Because if I don't, he'll ask me what I'm thinking. If he raises his voice, those around us will know. He'll start off by saying, "I shouldn't be eating this. It's full of carbs and salt and who knows what it has in it. I can taste the salt in it! Can you taste the salt in it? It's really salty. I can already feel my stomach bloating." He'll look down and pat his impossibly skinny stomach. I'll sit there choking down my food and looking down so I won't have to meet the eyes of the people looking at us. "Oh well," he might say, "I'll just work out a few more sets today." And I'll relax, thinking the tirade is over. But no such luck! God forbid he spills something on himself, or they get his order wrong. Then he'll stomp out to the car and he'll drive angrily home and he'll remain angry the rest of the day. My eyes will be red with unshed tears and he'll ask, "What's wrong Anna," hatefully. "Something is burning my eyes, that's all."

The Disappearing Penis, 1994

He is sure his penis is disappearing. And he insists it's broken. "Look," he says, holding it in his hand and bouncing it this way and that. "Doesn't it look crooked? It's broken." His eyes are wild and it registers in my mind again that he is becoming more irrational and more frightening. I don't know what to say. I start to reach out to touch his shoulder in comfort. He knocks my hand away. I feel I've entered the Twilight Zone when he insists, "It's true, you know. It's a fact that a penis can disappear. There's even a name for it."

That night he said he wanted to shoot a cop so the cop would shoot him. I knew he had pulled a gun on someone years before, but we didn't own a gun now. Then he told me that he was driving down the street the other day and saw a girl and he thought, "I should grab her and rape her." I decided I had to tell somebody. At work the next day I spoke with our legal liaison about George's behavior and his comments the day before. He advised me to get an ex parte issued. He explained that the court would send a process server to the house to serve the documents, which were basically an ultimatum that George either get counseling or get committed. I told George's mom I wanted to do that and she begged me not to. "He'll agree to counseling and won't go," she warned. I told her if he didn't, they would commit him. "Then he'll come back and take it out on us," she insisted.

"Okay," I thought. "But I'm going to leave. I won't be responsible for his harming someone else."

I often had nightmares, but one I never forgot, on February 8, 1994, felt like a nudge from my psyche that time was running out.

I entered a spinning elevator with George. It didn't go up and down but spun like a Tilt-a-whirl ride at a circus, only enclosed and without seats. It spun with enormous speed and jumping off would almost surely ensure death. George reached for the door and I begged him not to jump, but he was obstinate and made an unwise choice (like dad?). After he jumped I found myself kneeling beside his horribly broken body as he begged for help (like dad). My pity was mingled with a sad knowledge that I would have to take care of him now forever. I awoke thinking I would never escape. *"Why do I feel this unbearable weight of responsibility for an adult man who should not seem so helpless?"*

One Sunday during the Christmas season, our church put on a skit and a popular Christian actor was portraying Christ. I found myself watching him, my mind growing suspicious. Was he really the nice guy he seemed to be? Or did all men turn into monsters at home? Is he really like Christ, or do his wife and children fear him?

One evening we went to Hollywood Beach to walk on the boardwalk. The conversation was normal; he discussed what he needed to be doing and needed help with. I shook my head and occasionally commented just so he would think I was listening, but my mind was lost in a fantasy of walking along the beach with someone safe and loving. He was growing agitated and began needling me the rest of the evening, critically speaking my name like it tasted bad in his mouth:

"Anna, you're shaking your head no but saying yes;"

"Anna, I have no idea what you just said or what it meant. It doesn't even make sense. Your sentence structure is wrong and you used the wrong word, and don't use the word 'hate', it is not nice;"

"Anna, get your finger out of your mouth and don't touch your face. Who knows where your hands have been;"

"Anna, why are you fiddling with your hair again?"

That night, lying in bed, my mind began a familiar cycle as I calculated my age. If I left now, it might still be possible to meet someone and have a baby. But that wouldn't be possible for much longer. My dreams of having a child were quickly fading. I remembered the poem I had written the other day, as I sat on the porch:

I had taken a pad and pen outside, wanting to get away from George for a few minutes. I sat down on the porch stoop and berated myself for forgetting my house key. (George had locked me out a few times before.) I didn't hear the lock engage this time though, so I started writing about my imaginary little boy and a trip to the beach:

Little Boy Lost

If you were here with me, my little one,
we'd sit outside and watch the dying sun.
You're tired now, and quiet at my side
and teachable. We watch the ebbing tide.
The clouds have changed their patterns; we'll stay here
until the dark sky makes them disappear.
The birds are chirping, saying their goodnights

117

before they go to bed, rest from their flights.
We watch the darkening ocean, oh so vast,
and see in it the moon's reflection cast.
I teach you of God's touch in all the earth,
remind you that His world, and you, have worth.
Now all is dark, your sleepy little eyes
are heavy and your mind is void of "whys".
I gather you, so sandy from your wade,
knowing, today, that memories were made.
But wait, my eyes now open, you're not here.
My arms feel empty as I dry a tear.
I understand, so deep inside of me,
that you, my darling son, will never be.

Still thinking about my poem, unable to sleep, I wondered if I would ever hold a baby or comfort a toddler who has skinned his knee. I squeezed my eyes shut and tears escaped, running down and wetting my pillow. I reminded myself it was my fault. I could have left so long ago. Why hadn't I? Why couldn't I? What is the overpowering anxiety that keeps me trapped here? I have to find an answer. I've tried the church, my professors, counselors and friends. There has to be an answer, unless there is something wrong with me that is completely unique.

Looking up at the ceiling, I prayed, "God, if it is hopeless, please take one of us home. And I don't really care if I'm the one you take. I don't want to live like this anymore. I don't want to have to feel the iron strength of his muscles as I push against his arms when he has me against the wall. Help me find the courage within me to leave and tell me if it is okay with You if I do. Or else, please let me come home to You."

The next morning George's mom walked through the kitchen where he was. She had some dirty laundry to put in the garage, but he was convinced she was spying on him. After she walked out, I heard him calling her a jerk. I told him she could hear him and he said he didn't care. I told him he'd better care because she was providing us a place to live. He just walked away saying, "She's a jerk". His mom went into her room and closed the door softly, but it clicked. He jumped up and screamed, "That stinking cow! I'd like to slam her head in a door." He ran into the bathroom and slammed the door as hard as he could. His mom stuck her head out her bedroom door and mouthed, "Are you okay?" I shook my head yes even though I'm sure she thought I looked terrified. As he exited the bathroom, she closed the door again. "Click!"

May 1995

Around the summer of 1995 I began to take an interest in exercising. I think it was a need to feel some control over something again. George had always been on my case to exercise and it seemed like just another duty I had to perform for him. But I started doing it for me and it was different. For the first time in my life, I was beginning to feel good in my skin. I was not looking for attention, but I got positive feedback from some of the guys at work, which made me wonder if I was as unattractive as George led me to believe.

September 1996

I was thriving at my new job and George continued to monitor fire calls when it was convenient for him. I suspected he would never find a full time job. Finally, in 1996, things began to happen at home and at work.

Firefighters crave the adrenaline rush of a fire. They don't wish people harm, but they love to do what they were trained to do. George, however, slept through the biggest fire in the history of Plantation on September 6, 1996 when the Plantation Towne Mall caught fire consuming 56,000 square feet. When I called to see if he had responded, I woke him up. He walked to the living room window and he could see the smoke. I thought surely he'll drive over and help. But he didn't. The men in my squad could not believe George missed that fire because he was napping.

In September of 1996, after the Towne Mall fire, George accepted a full time position as an EMT with the Plantation Fire Department. I tried to feel optimistic, but I knew he preferred firefighting over medical work. Sure enough, he hated it. He felt stuck. And he became even more difficult to live with.

George's mother and I had visited the Vet Center in town. The counselor there likened his behavior to PTSD. When I mentioned he'd never seen battle, the counselor suggested personality disorders. He offered to meet with George, but I knew George would never go, and would be furious if he found out we had. George only visited doctors when he had to, or for bizarre ailments ("my hair hurts"). He was especially skeptical of and distrusted psychologists. That didn't surprise me; who wants to have their issues brought out into the light where they are forced to deal with them?

September 14, 1996, Life in "Crazy-ville"

One night George kept getting up to look out the window every few minutes, saying he heard something outside. When he left to go for a drive, I recorded in my journal how bizarre his behavior had been:

He's a study in contradictions.

It terrifies me to hear him talking to himself every time he walks in to another room. And he always sounds angry. Sometimes I'll hear him hit something with his fist, or throw something. Then he'll walk out of the room with a smile on his face. It's bizarre. Or else he'll seem fine when he goes in to the bathroom, and then walks out in a whole different demeanor, dark, angry and hostile.

Every time I go in to his mom's room he wants to know what's up, or what's wrong. Sometimes he's by the door when I walk out, as if he thinks we are talking about him. If I need to share a secret with her I'll quickly write it down, while in her room, and hand it to her, knowing he's listening. Whenever I talk to someone on the phone he wants to know who it was and what I was talking about. Sometimes I hear the click of the other extension pick up. I hate it when the phone rings and there's no one there. I know it's only telemarketers, but he thinks it's my "boyfriend".

121

*When I go somewhere he wants his mom to go with
me. If I go alone he checks the odometer to see if the
destination matches the mileage.*

*He's always hungry but never gains weight. He binges
and then complains about what he ate.*

*He's Jekyll and Hyde. He's the scariest person
I've ever met.*

While George was scary, he was also pitiful to me. Some part of
me longed to rescue him, to make him all better. I often felt he was
my child instead of my husband. I was the strong one in the relationship, although I never felt strong. I needed someone to be strong
for me and often felt I was ready to collapse from all the pressure.
But I was the one supporting us, and taking care of every aspect of
our lives. And I did this with no support from him, no rewards, no
show of affection or acknowledgement that I was of value to him.
But somehow the thought of leaving him made me feel as if I was a
mother leaving her child on the side of the road, abandoning him to
the elements and dangers of the world. If I had just understood then
that those were the same feelings I had experienced when my dad
was so pitiful and weak! Everything about our relationship was top-
sy-turvy and lopsided and all turned around. Behind all of the dysfunction was a fear of him because of his ever-present anger, control
and mental abuse.

PART III

Escape and Captured

The Journey

One day you finally knew
what you had to do, and began,
though the voices around you
kept shouting
their bad advice —
though the whole house
began to tremble
and you felt the old tug
at your ankles.
"Mend my life!"
each voice cried.
But you didn't stop.
You knew what you had to do,
though the wind pried
with its stiff fingers
at the very foundations,
though their melancholy
was terrible.
It was already late
enough, and a wild night,
and the road full of fallen
branches and stones.
But little by little,
as you left their voices behind,

the stars began to burn

through the sheets of clouds,

and there was a new voice

which you slowly

recognized as your own,

that kept you company

as you strode deeper and deeper

into the world,

determined to do

the only thing you could do —

determined to save

the only life you could save."

~ Mary Oliver ~[2]

Chapter 7

The New Guy...

I was getting interested in writing my story, hoping to garner some meaning out of all my years of confusion and wanting to help other women. At the same time I felt my body stirring with unexpressed and unsatisfied sexual feelings that were new to me. I was in my early 40s, but blooming like a teenager because, as a teen, I had suppressed all of those urges and feelings.

And so I found myself writing stories that combined truth and fiction. I would write about an actual experience with George and conclude it with a romantic or erotic tryst with an imaginary man. I wrote the stories for me, as an outlet, but let some of my girlfriends read them. I think my main motivation was to enlighten others to my plight and perhaps get encouragement and help to leave.

My friends began confessing they read the stories with their husbands and it "stirred things up". That wasn't my goal, but the transparency of sharing my pain would end up being a catalyst that led me to a person I never thought would end up being supportive.

Summer of 1996, Joel

God must have a sense of humor because one day, in early summer of 1996, my boss called me in to his office for a private chat. When he told me Joel was coming to our squad, he chuckled at the expression on my face.

"Why don't you like him, Anna? He's really a nice guy. He's one of my best friends."

I shared the rumors circulating about him, such as how he and his wife were swingers and took part in obscene sex acts and that he was crude and selfish. I mentioned that his secretary told me he did disgusting things, like removing his shoes and putting his stinky feet on his desk and brushing his teeth in the water fountain.

Again, sarge chuckled, telling me, "You can't believe all the things you hear. It will be okay."

I begged him to pick someone else, but the paperwork had gone through and his decision was final. He couldn't pass up a good detective just to please his wary secretary. Adding insult to injury, sarge put his desk right up against mine, separated only by a thin partition. My job had always been my haven, but I felt like my one safe place was being taken away. Again I approached my boss:

"Do you have to put him there? Can't you move somebody else there and put him somewhere else?"

"No," my boss chuckled. "I can't make somebody else move. Everyone likes where they are."

Since I had typed statements for Joel, I was already intimidated by him. He had accused me once of losing a cassette, and then had found it in his desk. But, like an oncoming locomotive, the force of Joel couldn't be stopped and he settled in, one day, on the other side of the partition in front of my desk. Unhappily I waited for the first shoe to fall…literally!

We didn't start out too well. One day as I followed him into the hallway he passed gas and I thought, "Darn, it's started already. Everything his secretary told me must be true." One day my boss asked me to call Joel's house on his day off. Joel wasn't home but his wife was. A few minutes later Joel called and yelled at me for waking up his wife, who worked nights. I'd only done what I was asked. His biting criticism had made me cry, as I thought sadly, "Another angry man in my life! And he hates me." Another scary man had invaded my one safe place in the world!

A Change of Heart

As the weeks passed I observed Joel and found that he had warmth about him when he talked about his children. I saw that he treated crime victims kindly and then I heard he was active in his church. I grew more impressed with him as time went by. Okay, maybe he wasn't so bad. But I still thought he disliked me. After working a security detail at the Olympics in Atlanta from July 19 to August 4, he returned with gifts for everyone in the squad except me. And he never said much to me. It was like he never knew I existed except when he needed his tapes transcribed.

In time we did start talking more and became friendlier. One day I had a panic attack after George screamed at me over the phone. I couldn't breathe well and started hyperventilating, so I quickly dialed our bureau receptionist. My boss was out so the captain ran in with a paper bag for me to breathe in. He sat me down in sarge's office, confiding that his ex-wife had been mentally ill. He shared that he had tried hanging in there with her for years and finally had to save himself. He encouraged me to get some help and get free.

The captain left and I returned to my desk, realizing that Joel had quietly slipped in to the squad and had observed the whole episode. I remembered he had said something to me earlier and might think he had upset me. I quietly explained my being upset had nothing to do with him. He *had been* concerned, and was impressed that I was sensitive enough to take the time and offer him an explanation. He was also clearly touched to find out about my trials at home. We started talking more after that.

I was surprised to find that Joel was easy to talk to and that he felt safe. Knowing he was a Christian helped. One day he told me about something that happened at the Olympics. He said a female officer had come on to him there. Later I walked up to him when no one else was around. "That woman who came on to you, you didn't, did you?" He laughed and said no and told me he was a one woman man. I felt relieved. He seemed like a man who could be trusted. I was thankful he resisted the brazen woman's come-on. He was still the man I thought he was. He hadn't disappointed me.

In time I came to view Joel as a friend. He asked why I had been so upset about him coming to the squad and, when I told him, he laughed. He knew about the rumors that circulated and he was the type of person who didn't really care what people thought about him. In fact, he thought it was funny.

I opened up to him more about my life and one day mentioned my stories. I had let another male detective read one and was disappointed that he only focused on the erotic aspects. Joel asked if he could read a story and I anxiously awaited his response. After he read it, his reaction was nothing like the other detective's. He didn't even mention the erotic part, but seemed genuinely touched by my issues with George.

Since he reacted that way, I started asking questions about what men really want and like, since I felt I had failed miserably. He answered every question and, as he did, I began to accept that the problem wasn't me but George. What a relief!

One day Joel confided to me that he was not as happy as he seemed. In fact he was seriously unhappy and had decided, before he even knew me, that he was leaving someday. He was building a boat, but no one took him seriously when he talked about sailing away. He shared his reasons for wanting to leave and it sounded like he had Biblical grounds. Rather than the typical line of "my wife doesn't understand me," he spoke well of her, stating she was a wonderful mother and that he wanted to stay until his children were grown because it was difficult to raise children alone. When he mentioned he had wanted to work things out with her until the church gave her some bad advice, it touched a familiar chord of empathy in me. I knew much about the church failing people who fell outside the accepted norm.

Joel's best friend was also in our squad. He noticed Joel and I talking more and told Joel that he thought I was looking for someone to rescue me. The exact opposite was true. I wanted desperately to be strong enough to leave and get out on my own. I wanted to rescue myself and then meet someone who would really love me and treat me well, if I could ever trust again.

I'm not sure if sharing our personal pain was a betrayal to our spouses. It's something I have often wondered about. But I do know that we had both decided to leave our marriages before we allowed our feelings to grow for each other. I never dreamed I would fall for a married man, especially one who had small children, because it went against everything I believed.

One night George was working and his mom was away when the phone rang. It was Joel, asking me to step out and look in the mailbox. He said he would hold on while I did. I had on my robe and had been folding clothes in the living room, but I darted out to the mailbox and found a small paper bag from Cracker Barrel. Inside was a golf-sized orange ball with a smiley face. When I picked the phone back up, I was laughing. He asked if he could come in and promised to only stay a minute. After hesitating a second, I said okay because he'd given me no reason to distrust him.

When Joel walked in, I thanked him for the gift and then he did something totally unexpected. He asked me if he could just hold me for a minute. He never made a move toward me until I said, "Okay". He walked over slowly and gently put his arms around me and just held me. I remember thinking that it was the warmest thing I'd ever felt in my life. He held me like he valued me; then, as he had promised, he stepped back and headed for the door.

I had told Joel about my "beagle incident" and he had shared he was building himself a boat. Soon we began writing a story together, about life on a boat and a beagle named Charlie. We took turns writing chapters, as the story became longer. Soon our story took a turn, delving in to the physical.

I found myself aroused when I was around Joel or even when I thought about him, something I had not experienced when I dated George. I had never experienced such deep feelings before. They were so powerful it was almost scary. I know it sounds like a cliché, but I felt I was awaking from a long, dark sleep, wonderfully alive and in touch with my own body and sensuality.

I was not ready to carry our relationship into the physical realm yet and thought about the few guys at work who had come on to me before. Joel was not like them, but I did not want to have a physical relationship with someone I didn't love and had no hope of a future with.

Fall 1997, Cans in the Dryer

George's diet was a constant source of stress. I often thought of scriptures I had read about what goes into our body not being a problem, but what comes out (our words and actions), another about bodily exercise profiting little and yet another about those whose god is their belly (scriptures referenced are Mt. 15:11; 1 Tim. 4:8; Phil. 3:19, New International Version). Clearly George's priorities were twisted. I would not have minded helping him with his diet if he was sick and needed a special diet. I would have dealt with his OCPD and even been willing to support us and remain poor if he had a legitimate disability. I have a never-ending supply of love and patience, but everything George did was coupled with such wrath that I was constantly scared for my life and safety.

One day, George would want beans added to his diet—not just one type, but two. "And don't make too many. Only cook a quarter cup of each." He didn't care how much work went in to it. He knew I had to soak them overnight or boil them for two minutes and then let them sit for an hour. It meant two dirty pots and the use of electricity for a tiny amount of beans; and then, the next day, he would decide he had a food allergy to beans and I would have to make something different. I'd tell him I would eat the beans, but I'd take them to work and toss them out. If I'd eaten all the beans I told him I would eat, I'd have probably contributed to global warming!

One day he wanted orange juice so I bought him some. The next day he said he had a reaction to the orange juice, but wanted to try cranberry juice. He didn't want food thrown out, but I couldn't eat all of his "change of mind foods" and I threw out so much I could have probably fed a family for a year. Some days he wanted cheese, so I'd go to the Deli. He demanded salt free, fat free cheese. I could only find low sodium, low fat (he was impossibly skinny anyhow) so I asked for a separate bag to wrap it in, swapping packages when I got to the car. If he was waiting in the car, I would quickly change the wrappers in line, which annoyed those waiting behind me.

I know this seems deceitful, but I honestly felt I had no choice. I was too afraid to stand up to him because his temper tantrums were terrifying and I always felt he was on the verge of beating me to a pulp. My attempts at reasoning with him were never met with success, only more anger and hostility.

When George was in "bean mode" I would often buy cans of beans and sneak them into the kitchen and hide them behind other cans where his mom kept her food, or in her room. When he was in the bathroom I would grab two cans of beans, open them, and pour them in to containers quickly, or rush the cans in to his mom, where she kept a can opener. Sometimes I would leave them with her and she would open them and put them into the plastic containers, and I would run into her room and get them when he was occupied. Whoever opened the cans had the task of disposing of them. If it was his mom, she would throw them away on one of her outings. If it was me, I had a routine worked out:

132

My heart racing, I would sneak into the garage, off the kitchen, wrap the empty cans in a plastic bag and stick them in the dryer. I couldn't put them in the trash can because he went through the trash.

One day I forgot the cans in the dryer and he found them. He stormed into the kitchen demanding to know why the cans were in the dryer. I froze. His mom happened to walk in to the kitchen at that time and took the fall for me, stating she meant to take them to the trash and joking about having a senior moment.

People often told me George's mom should stand up for me more or make him leave. Others, even George's ex-girlfriend Sarah, understand that he had a way of manipulating women that used fear, intimidation, control and neediness to cause debilitating confusion and helplessness. It's like a private "George club" of women who have an underlying current of understanding that only abused women can grasp. His mom and I became close as we strove to survive him together.

I substituted many food items, but most of them were in paper or cardboard wrappers and could be more easily camouflaged with other garbage. I was just too tired to make everything from scratch and cooking the way he demanded was sometimes impossible. He wouldn't accept that some ingredients cannot be deleted, but have to be substituted. I substituted what I could, choosing more healthy alternatives, but I couldn't leave out oil altogether in some recipes, or some type of sweetener in desserts. And he changed his mind daily about what he could and couldn't eat, and I do mean daily!

So I lived in a state of hypervigilance, rushing around and sneaking and making promises and trying to fulfill them. I made phone calls for him, looked up information, made his doctor appointments, did laundry on certain days and shopped on certain days and took his mom with me everywhere. I dressed and walked and ate and combed my hair a certain way. I died more and more and became a mini-George and lost track of who I really was. And then, I just couldn't anymore.

And I began to rebel.

The actual dryer in the George's mom's garage.

October 12, 1997, The Tryst

George's mom was completely retired now and always at home, which George hated. He was more and more miserable as an EMT. He had become interested in a Clinical Pastoral Education (CPE) program in North Carolina in 1996, after beginning work as an EMT. It was close to where our friends Warren and Lois lived. He had applied for the next program and started sending 250 dollars a month to hold a house near the hospital, hoping he was accepted. The program next started in September of 1998, so he sent 250 dollars a month for two years to hold the house. If approved, George would be leaving for North Carolina.

I did not want to be responsible for breaking up a home, but Joel had convinced me he was leaving before I entered the picture. I'd like to say we waited to further our relationship, but we didn't. Our first tryst was in Joel's van late one evening while George was at work and his mom was away. Looking back, the chance I took is frightening. I risked it because I longed to finally know how it felt to be wanted. I think most women who engage in affairs are looking for love and a sense of self-worth.

As I stepped out of his van after that first time together, I turned around and said, "I love you, but no promises" because I still wasn't sure of our future. The following day I received flowers. The note simply said "Thank you!" and that small bouquet of flowers meant more to me than anything George had ever given me. George had often said that flowers are a waste of money because they die. But flowers are romantic and the memory of them lasts forever. I have pictures of every bouquet Joel has ever given me.

Having never been with anyone but George, I wasn't sure how to interpret my feelings. The day after our tryst, the day I received the flowers, I went home and changed for a run. I went to a small park closer to home, right behind the fire station where George was stationed. It started raining gently as I began running. My emotions were in a jumble and I prayed as I ran, my tears of anguish mixing with the raindrops. I wondered if God would even hear me because of what I had done, but I prayed anyhow. Surely He did not approve, but I felt He understood. I didn't feel condemned, but loved. I didn't feel God's anger, but His sadness. It was like He was hurting and crying with me and for me, and the raindrops were His tears.

The only man in the world I had wanted did not really want me, but someone else did. The man I chose for life, who should have loved me as Christ loved the church, frightened me so much that he pushed me right in to someone else's arms, being a catalyst for my setting aside my own personal convictions. I was not blaming George for what I'd done. I knew I was responsible for my actions. But I also understood my fear, desperation and my need for hope and reassurance that I was worthy of love.

The rain stopped and, thankful to be alone in the park, I sat on a bench and held my head in my hands. I was torn and had a vivid memory of the night, long ago, in a Dairy Queen parking lot when mom and dad tugged at me, each trying to take me away from the other. Behind me was someone who drained the life out of me and terrified me and yet somehow made me feel responsible for him. In front of me was warmth, light, strength and love in a man who wanted to take care of *me*. With all of his criticism and hostility, George still made me feel he would be lost without me. But I was lost *with* him!

I looked up at the gray sky, hugging myself, and felt a warmth flood over me as I imagined God holding me in His arms. Could I have been wrong all those years about Him? Could it be that He loved me still? Was there something going on that seemed too much to hope for? Could He be working in my life and Joel's, bringing us both the love we'd searched for all of our lives? If so, could we be together without his children being damaged? What about his wife? Did she really not love him? What would happen to George and should I care?

The small park where I went to run and the bench I sat on, occupied by George's mom and Charlie years later.

A Magical Time

When I dated George he had always seemed unsure of our relationship. I never felt I was a prize that he longed to win as his precious wife. Joel was so different. He heaped little gifts on me, and numerous cards that made me feel special for the first time in my life. He pursued me, making me feel pretty and even sexy. Most of all I felt loved, wanted and valued for all of me. I truly felt treasured.

One Sunday George was working and his mom let me borrow her car. I met Joel at a local hotel on a rainy day. I remember walking through the lobby feeling very grown up and sophisticated. For a lady in my 40s, I was definitely a late bloomer. Joel had said he wanted to watch me undress. I think I got one stocking off when he said, "Come here" and pulled me on to the bed with him. He just held me for a moment, and then he began to undress me. I had never been undressed before. I felt like I was experiencing love the way it was supposed to be and I was wishing my wedding night had been like this. It was like a beautiful dream. When Joel told me I was beautiful, I felt he really meant it. He held me for a while as if I was a long-sought treasure. Only then did he slowly make love to me, literally taking my breath away. And then he held me and slept as I listened to the rain hit the window and to his gentle snoring.

When he awoke he talked, sharing intimate details about his life. He expressed amazement that George could treat me so badly when, to him, I was so sweet. I replied that one man's trash was another man's treasure and that to George I was nothing special. I had not been the woman he really wanted. "You're my little treasure," Joel said. From that time on he called me his little treasure and told me I had saved him from a life of incredible sadness and loneliness.

When I got home that night, I felt empty and lonely. I had left the arms of an incredible man who cherished me and had returned to a cold house where no love existed. I wondered what was going to happen now. Dad and George had failed and harmed me. Joel was now my hero. I knew trust would come hard for me, but I had a feeling Joel would never hurt or disappoint me.

August 1998, A Taste of Freedom

George and I made a trip to North Carolina, staying with Lois and Warren, so George could be interviewed for the CPE Program. While George was gone to his interview, I told our friends about his worsening anger. I also told them about Joel and shared some things about his situation.

Warren pastored a conservative Pentecostal church and I knew he would be concerned about me falling in love with a married man. His compassion was a wonderful surprise. He told me there was a woman in his church in the same situation and he could not advise her to stay in an abusive marriage.

Warren explained that the New Testament word for divorce means "to tear apart, to break down" and reminded me that this is what George had done to our marriage by his despicable behavior. He talked about how spouses are to build each other up, choose each other above all, and give themselves completely to each other, welcoming affection and not tearing each other down, or denying affection to each other (1 Cor. 7:5).

Warren surprised me further by praying over me, even thanking God for bringing Joel in to my life to give me love and courage and hope. I felt relief that someone who had witnessed George's anger was validating my wish to be separated from him and was assuring me of God's continued love and grace. I understood that Warren was not condoning sin, but I felt he was convinced God would not reject me for escaping an abusive marriage.

Not long after we returned home George got an acceptance letter from the CPE instructor. I went to work the next day giddy with joy that he would be leaving, giving me the opportunity to find a lawyer and hopefully keep him from returning. Joel chuckled when he saw how happy I was.

Chapter 8

...Captures My Heart

September 1998

eorge was gone. I was free! For the first few weeks I would go out alone in his mom's car and just drive around, relishing being able to go where I wanted. My whole demeanor changed and I felt hopeful about my future. "This is the real Anna," I thought.

Joel had to attend a two-week training course in Alabama and he asked me to accompany him. It was a wonderful two weeks that ended much too soon. I could tell Joel missed his children terribly, and when he spoke with his wife on the phone, I wondered if he still harbored feelings for her as well. One night I grabbed a blanket and sat on the floor to do some soul searching. When Joel awoke he thought I was a sad sight, in his mind the poster child of an abused woman. He called me back to bed and cuddled me. He could tell I had been crying and I finally said what was bothering me.

"You're not ready to leave yet are you?"

He hesitated a moment and then admitted, "No."

I was heartbroken, yet thankful for his honesty. Now at least I knew where I stood and that I needed to face the fact that I was alone. As we got closer to home, I couldn't stop the tears because I felt we were coming to an end.

When Joel dropped me off I saw that the hurricane shutters were still over the windows of George's mom's house, from a recent hurricane threat. I knew the house would be dark and claustrophobic. Joel sat my luggage on the porch and left, anxious to get home and see his girls. The hurricane threat was over, so I immediately got some tools and took down the shutters, storing them in the garage. Then I began unpacking.

Joel had given me a pager for my last birthday, so that we could send secret numeric codes to each other. When it started going off every few minutes I ignored it, even when his home number appeared in it. Later the phone rang and, not having caller I.D., I answered.

"I got home and they said hi and then they left for a horse show," Joel sad sadly. I told him I was sorry. Then he asked if he could pick me up the next morning. He wanted to give me lessons on driving his stick-shift Jeep. I had misgivings, but I agreed. I still wasn't sure what to do about us. I had even considered seeking a transfer to another part of the city.

I was still unpacking when there was a knock at the door. I peeked through the shades and saw a boy holding flowers and a flower delivery truck in the street. I took the flowers and thanked him, assuming they were from Joel. When I saw they were from George my heart sank. He only sent them because he was away from me and sensed he was losing me. As I dropped them in the trash can the phone rang. It was George, calling to give me a shopping list of things he needed me to buy and mail to him.

Joel picked me up the next morning and gave me a lesson in driving the Jeep. Before he took me home, he tried to think of somewhere I could live. I told him he couldn't take care of everyone, and he asked, "Why not?"

The following weekend George came home, informing his mom and me that Mark, his supervisor, had diagnosed him with Obsessive Compulsive Personality Disorder, a different form of OCD. He gave us reading material that described George very well. However, it didn't cover the anger and abuse, two characteristics I knew George would never let Mark see.

Once George left I went back to formulating my plan. I was not certain when Joel planned to leave and I did not want to pressure him, but I knew what I wanted and needed to do. I penned a letter to Mark in North Carolina, informing him of George's anger and abuse and of my desire to leave him. Since he'd had time to observe George, I asked for his advice about the best way to tell George, and asked if we could talk. Then I waited nervously for his call.

About a week later Mark phoned me. We spoke for almost an hour and then he asked for a little time to consider the best way I could handle telling George I wanted to leave. Before hanging up he mentioned a wonderful poem by Mary Oliver called "The Journey" and asked me to look it up and read it. He never tried talking me out of leaving George and I think, by him mentioning the poem, he was letting me know, in a subtle way, that I was probably doing what was best for me.

The next time George came home he arrived angry, with notes he needed typed. His yelling caused his mom to stick her head out of her bedroom door to check on me. He told her to mind her business and she backed into her room and closed the door. Then said he was going back to North Carolina, announcing:

"I'm telling you goodbye now because I almost got in a wreck on the way down, so this might be the last time you see me."

Then he stormed out, slamming the door and burned rubber pulling out of the driveway. I was still sitting on the couch, afraid to move, when his mom tiptoed out of her room. I explained what had happened and what he'd said about the car wreck that almost happened. We both said the same thing at the same time:

"It couldn't be that easy."

Less than five minutes later George pulled into the driveway again and walked into the house, finding me still sitting in the same spot. He stayed the whole weekend, angry the whole time.

George's CPE program was going to end on December 14, leaving me nearly four months to prepare. Mark had phoned me a second time, advising me not to talk to George face to face, but to write him a letter and send it to his office and he would read it to George, offering him emotional support. He thought that way would be safer for me. He also advised waiting until near the end of the program since I was petrified George would pack up and come right home, even though I was requesting, in the letter, that he remain in North Carolina. My fears were realized when George announced he was coming home. Apparently he was not going to honor my request, and thought he could come back and change my mind.

December 1998

When I found out George was not going to stay in North Carolina, I had to find an apartment very quickly. I had forgotten it was snow bird season, and very few rentals were available, at least that I could afford. I finally found a small apartment, attached to a house, in Plantation. It wasn't ready to be inhabited, however. Tree roots were growing under the bathroom cabinets and shower floor. The whole bathroom had to be redone. George was due to come home so I packed my things and got a storage unit. The day of his arrival I had a suitcase beside my desk and no idea where to go. I decided I would sleep at my desk that night.

I called George's mom later and she said that George had come home with all kinds of gifts for me, including a life sized stuffed lion. She said when he saw my things gone he began to cry, telling her he had lost his best friend. He had expected I would wait until he came back to move out, giving him time to change my mind. I knew I couldn't do that because he would cry and play on my sympathy, and make promises to change, causing that awful dark anxiety to rise up in me again.

Sure enough, he called me before the end of the work day and could hardly talk for crying. "Can't you just come home and let us talk?" I told him no, I was afraid of him. "Well would you meet me somewhere then?" I told him no, that a friend was letting me stay at her house and was waiting for me in the car. "You'll go home with a friend but won't talk to your own husband?" he asked. My heart sank as I realized I shouldn't have waited so long to find a place to live.

"Why did he have to come back?" I wondered. I told him I'd call him when I got to work the next day and hung up. Then I prepared to settle in for the night, hoping nobody would walk into the squad and see me there and wonder why I hadn't gone home. The next day a coworker informed me she had a spare bedroom I could stay in until the apartment was ready.

George continued to beg me to come home. I knew he would never change and I had no love left for him. The many times he'd frightened me and made me cry he always had one of two responses: "You'll get over it" or "If you don't like it, you can leave." I don't think he believed I ever really would. Besides I was in love with Joel now, and hoped he and I could have a life together.

Joel told me he knew it took a lot of courage to leave, and that he was proud of me. I remember thinking, "If you knew how frightened and confused I am inside, you might not be so proud of me." I had left physically, but I was an emotional wreck. I felt like a bird with no place to land, like the one Noah sent from the ark. I was flying around in a world of darkness and my wings were growing so tired. Physically I was exhausted. Each time I walked outside, I looked over my shoulder to see if George had followed me. And he continued to phone my desk, leaving messages that begged me to give him another chance.

As long as George had been far away I relished my freedom and felt fine. Having him in close proximity was far too much of a threat. At work I felt safe, knowing he couldn't get to me. When I finally moved in to the apartment, however, I realized emotional support was lacking. George's mom was afraid to come and visit me, lest he follow her or get angry at her for being welcome when he wasn't. My friends were all married and, considering me now single, really didn't spend time with me away from work. Joel saw me when he could, but I still felt unsure of his plans or intentions about us.

Joel and I had kept our affair a secret. One day another detective gave me a ride to the bank to cash my check. Sitting across from me he shocked me. "You drive me crazy, you know. I'd love to see you. I know I could trust you to be discreet. Could I have a key to your apartment?" I was extremely uncomfortable. First of all, no man other than Joel had been "crazy about me" and this man admitted he only wanted a mistress, not to leave his wife. This man and George had both asked for keys; no one got a key except Joel.

I had taken enough money from our savings to open an account, put the down payment on the apartment and purchase a car. I guess I appeared to be fine to everyone. But I wasn't. I couldn't relax because the man who had done the apartment repairs had stolen some of my underwear, broken dishes and used food items. I was afraid he had made himself a key and might come in on me one night. It was difficult to sleep and I was lonely. Sometimes I would go to work and just sit at my desk on the weekend. Then another complication arose; I found out I needed surgery.

*In my traffic controller uniform beside my first new car,
looking confident and feeling anything but!*

When George had been gone I felt confident. With him back I felt strangely fearful of making decisions. In some way I felt I still needed his permission to do things. These feelings shamed and confused me and had nothing to do with loving George. With him back in town, I didn't feel free anymore. I knew I had an issue with men, especially those in authority or power over me. In college, my counselor had hinted at my past. Now my counselor, Roberta, at Women in Distress was delving into my past as well. She asked me to write out my feelings about my dad, further fueling my suspicion there was something important I needed to address.

Since men at work had approached me, I began to realize I was uncomfortable saying "no" to them, feeling like I had no personal power. When they came on to me, I'd offer an excuse to walk away quickly, rather than just saying I wasn't interested. Then I would avoid them. Joel was the only exception. I had never felt powerless with him, but felt free to be myself. Maybe I sensed that Joel had my interests at heart, not only his.

1999, Humiliation of Failure

When Joel had told me how proud he was of me, how courageous I was, I smiled. But the real Anna was hiding from him. I felt stupid for not preparing better. I felt flawed because, instead of being excited to get away, I felt miserable. I wanted to be brave and strong, tried putting on a brave front for everyone, and tried ignoring George's constant begging, wondering why his anguish made me feel so miserable. I wanted to be okay, but I wasn't.

Joel did his best to support me, having his own family issues to work out as well. One day I went home to my apartment and thought I saw Joel's van parked down the street. Walking in my door, I found my computer hooked up and the fan on above it and it felt a little homier. I was touched that he had done that for me. One night he came over late to put a lock on my gate so that I would feel safer.

Before leaving for home each day, Joel would meet me in the stair well and give me a long hug and kiss. Then I watched him drive away, envying the wife he was going home to. "Does she know how blessed she is?" I wondered, "Will he ever come home to me?"

More complications arose when I had my shoulder checked for constant pain. I had a torn rotator cuff in my left shoulder. Therapy didn't help so I would have to have surgery, not arthroscopic, but major surgery because I needed bone removed. I would need assistance after surgery and wouldn't be able to drive. There was no one to help except George's mom. It seemed my only option was to move back with her while I underwent therapy. Joel said at least he wouldn't have to worry about my being alone. George's mom promised to pay close attention and, if she felt I was threatened, would phone 911 immediately.

George had gone back to the Fire Department, tail tucked between his legs, and asked for his EMT job back. No way did they want him back, but they did say he could volunteer as a firefighter again. I chose a night he was in training to move my things back in to his mom's house. Joel and his friend helped me. Joel could read me well and sensed that I felt like a failure. "Don't worry," he assured me, "things will work out."

When George came in that night and saw my things, he felt I was coming back to him. When I didn't go to bed with him that night, opting to sleep on the air mattress in the living room, he was disappointed. But he was on best behavior for a while, hoping he could change my mind. In spite of the repercussions to her, mom made numerous trips out of her bedroom to keep an eye on me. Joel picked me up each morning for work and then dropped me off on his way home. The air mattress would come in handy later on, when I visited mom and cooked for her on some nights when Joel was staying with his children.

On the air mattress with Charlie at George's mom's house.

Although George was trying to be on good behavior, his true nature always won out. I had expected George's mom would prepare my food after surgery, but George wouldn't let her. When he made me a sandwich he would throw it on the table in front of me, like someone begrudgingly tossing scraps to a dog. I hated feeling at his mercy and couldn't wait to be gone again.

Around this time I found out my brother was in a coma. He passed away a few weeks later. Over the next eight years, I lost my stepmother and the rest of my immediate family. My sister, my dad and my mother all passed away, leaving me the lone survivor of my immediate family. Thankfully I still have my step-sister.

My brother and sister never reached the age of 60. I feel their deaths are partly a result of the neglect and lack of nurturing they received as children, as well as the trauma and lack of stability.

149

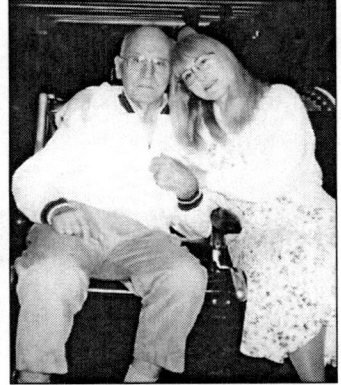

**With my mom, sister and brother, our last time together;
in the airport with dad, waiting to fly back to
Fort Lauderdale after a visit.**

Once I healed I had to find somewhere to live again. Would I succeed this time? Roberta, at Women in Distress, had told me that rarely did a client leave successfully the first time. She even had one who left seventeen times before she was successful.

Joel was moving his family in to another house closer to horse camp. When I told George's mom, she asked if he was moving with them. "I guess so," I replied. She told me she didn't understand why he would move with them if he wanted to be with me, and encouraged me to think about that.

Joel's Surprise

Not long after Joel had moved his family, he came to my desk and said he wanted to show me a surprise during our lunch break. I was curious all morning. When lunch time finally came, Joel drove me to an apartment complex in Plantation. He took my hand and led me up to a door. I wondered if he had borrowed someone's apartment for a tryst until we walked in and I saw it was empty. Then he turned me to face him and took both my hands in his.

"Whenever you are ready, I'll be here waiting for you."

He had found us a place to live together! The ramifications were clear to me; he had chosen a life with me.

George had accepted a position as a TSA at Fort Lauderdale/ Miami International Airport. That meant he would be able to support himself when I moved out this time. He was due to start work the next day and I planned on packing and moving my things out while he was at work that weekend, so he wouldn't hassle me. That night as I washed dishes he announced he was going out for a while. When he returned he said he had turned in his gear, declining the position. I was disgusted and asked him why. "I read their policies. If I make one little mistake I can be arrested. I don't need that kind of pressure." When he went to bed that night, I slipped three dresses in to my car trunk. I'd work out how to get the rest of my things later. The next day I met George's mom in the parking lot of Publix with a letter for George, telling him he needed to find a job and take care of himself. And I went "home" to Joel. I wouldn't get the remainder of my possessions from George's mom's house until August of 2014.

That night I lay in bed in front of our open window on my belly, my head resting in my hands, looking outside as the daylight faded. Joel lay beside me reading. When I looked up, he was watching me. "The way you look, lying there, all relaxed, is a memory I'll always treasure" he said. I wasn't alone. I had the love and support I needed. This time I would make it. But I had one more trial to overcome first.

Injustice

One morning I was getting ready for work. Joel had spent the night with his children and I would meet him at work. I got paged to call George's mom's house and dialed her number, expecting her to answer. Instead George answered. The last time I had spoken to him it was amicable and I had felt relaxed and happy, knowing my last hurdle had been overcome. He had assured me he was ready to move on with his life and I had offered to find an attorney and start proceedings. I'd even offered generously that I hoped we could be friends. But now George was crying. "I just can't move on," he said. "I just want to die. There's nothing else to live for now." I had felt so carefree and hopeful only a moment before and now I felt I'd been dropped out of a plane and was falling thousands of feet into a bottomless abyss. On some level I understood my emotional reaction was extreme but, nevertheless, it was real.

For a moment I felt disconnected from everything around me and I couldn't even hear his voice anymore. I slowly hung up the phone and just sat in the floor, too overcome with emotion to even cry. I felt a dark cloud loom over me, so heavy and real and I could almost see it. I had only experienced that dark cloud one other time in my life and my mind frantically began seeking that other experience so that I could find some clarity and explanation for what was happening. But, try as I might, I couldn't quite place it. I started shaking and thought about calling Joel but I knew he was in some type of training that day. I think I would have been better off had George screamed at me angrily because I was used to seeing him like that.

I called my boss and told him I couldn't come in and then I called my co-worker. When I told her what had happened she asked if I'd like her to come and pick me up for lunch. I said yes, that would be great. I figured if I could just talk it out with her it would lose its hold over my emotions. What happened next I can only assume was the result of a miscommunication. Perhaps when I told her George said there was nothing to live for, she misunderstood and thought I was saying that about me.

A few moments after I hung up with my friend, my boss phoned and said that he and my friend's boss were coming over. When they arrived they asked me to get in my car and follow them across the street to the park so we could talk. I wondered if I was in trouble for taking the day off. We sat at a picnic table and they asked what was going on, that my friend had feared I was suicidal. I explained about George's call and said I wasn't suicidal. They still wanted me to talk to the police psychologist, stating perhaps I needed some support until I got my divorce. I agreed and drove to his office, with them following me.

I assumed I would speak with the psychologist and then go on to work. I had met him a few years prior, when I went to talk to him about George. The psychologist suggested I might benefit from anti-depression medication while I went through the divorce pro- cess and sent me to a psychiatrist on our insurance plan, because only a psychiatrist can prescribe drugs. He assured me that I'd be surprised how many police officers took meds for anxiety, and that it was nothing to be ashamed of. He even admitted that he had bouts of depression. I didn't think I was depressed, but I said I'd go. That's where everything went horribly wrong.

It seemed the whole work day was wasted, but I expected to get a prescription and be home before Joel. I knew that my boss and my friend's boss had asked Joel what was going on with me, so I was anxious to assure him everything was fine and to explain what had happened. As I drove to the doctor's office, I was planning on what I'd make for dinner that night.

When the psychiatrist asked me why I was there I explained the whole situation to him, telling him that the police psychologist thought I might benefit from medicine for depression while I went through divorce proceedings. I still didn't think I suffered from depression, but I decided not to mention that. I could get a prescription, but I didn't have to take it.

Instead of accepting my reality and experience and being concerned that I was a victim of domestic abuse, he shocked my socks off by telling me I was depressed because I was having an affair, that divorce and adultery were both sins, no matter what the reason, and that I needed to go back to my husband. "You're depressed because you are not right with God." I was so appalled by his unprofessionalism and hurt by his judgment that I immediately broke down. I should have fought back, telling him he had no right to make moral judgments and that I was glad God wasn't like him. But I was too beaten down to even think of taking up for myself. His demeanor reeked of disgust and I think his next action was to punish me. He asked if I ever wanted to die. I was beginning to feel angry and I blurted out, "No but you are making me feel that way. Dying would be better than living with George." He stepped out again and when he came back he told me I could not leave.

So many times I've wished that I had told him I wanted to go to the restroom and just left. But this authority figure told me to stay put, that a deputy was coming to escort me to the hospital. "You want anti-depression meds? You can go to the depression ward for a few days." I suddenly had an image of dad being taken away in the ambulance, and everything felt surreal. Surely this was a nightmare and I'd awaken to find it was morning.

I still feel intense shame over this. I kept wondering, as I sat there and then took the ride in the back of a sheriff cruiser, what Joel would think of me. That was my main concern. If this leaked out, he would surely be embarrassed. Maybe he'd wonder what he'd gotten himself into with me. I had found the treasure I had been searching for my entire life. Would I lose him now because I went to the wrong doctor? Why did it seem fate was fighting me every step of the way? Was God disappointed in me? Was the psychiatrist right? Was I a sinful, bad, stupid woman who was being punished by God, or was the psychiatrist wrong and out of line, having no real understanding of God's mercy and grace? Could God be working behind the scenes, holding me in His hands through this storm? Had He sent Joel in to my life as my guardian angel? I felt that if Joel still wanted me after this, then he surely really loved me.

God can work even bad things out for our good. The deputy refused to handcuff me and he gently asked me to get in the back seat, then he asked me what had happened. He commented that it sounded like my husband was the one who should be Baker Acted, not me. When we got to the hospital I saw him speak to the intake nurse. When she took me back to strip search me, she only had me undress to my underwear and turn around once and then let me get dressed again. I asked to use the phone and called Joel and then called my boss's phone to let him know I needed some sick time.

The irony of the injustice overwhelmed me. George had been diagnosed with a mental disorder and had abused me for years, and I was only trying to escape his cruelty. Yet here *I* was being treated like a criminal while he sat at home, free to do as he wished.

My consult with the staff psychiatrist the next morning was short. He looked at me and asked what I was doing there. My blood screen was squeaky clean, yet he noticed my hands never stopped shaking. "What are you so afraid of?" he asked. After we talked awhile he said he was changing the forced order to a voluntary one, so it wouldn't be on my record. He said I could leave whenever I wanted, that I didn't belong there, and that *George* did. Then he suggested I make a formal complaint against the psychiatrist and to let Risk Management know about his conduct. He offered the option of my staying the three days allotted by insurance, saying he would meet with me daily and that he thought he could help me. He reminded me that George could not see me or phone me while I was there and the reprieve might be nice. I had plenty of sick time so I agreed.

This doctor was the first to offer me professional validation and keen insight. He described Joel's appearance and personality perfectly, before I even described him, saying I had made a wise choice. He said many women choose another abuser but that I had chosen someone completely different, indicating I truly wanted to be free from abuse. He offered me a prescription but said I would probably only need it until I knew George was completely out of my life and I was safe. The doctor made me feel smart and capable of making good decisions. After all, I had seen something in Joel that was special.

My suspicions about my difficulties were also validated when the doctor had me do a mental exercise in which I pictured myself walking away from George, him getting smaller in the background, and walking toward Joel. He noticed I was looking anxious and asked me what I was picturing. I told him instead of picturing myself getting happier, I was picturing George in horrific pain. The anxiety was almost overwhelming. It felt as if a force I couldn't name was keeping me tied to him. The doctor set aside his notebook and leaned closer to me. "Have you ever explored the relationship with your parents, especially your father, in relation to that anxiety you feel toward George?" He suggested I explore that further and offered his counseling services even after I left. "There is more going on here than depression. And give yourself more credit. You are very courageous. You are a survivor."

Joel was with his children the night I left the hospital, so I called George's mom to pick me up. Instead, George showed up. He took me to Walgreen's before taking me to his mom's house where my car was. The whole way to the drug store and then to his mom's house he screamed at me. "Don't ever threaten to call someone when I talk about suicide anymore. I'll tell them you're lying and that *you're* the one wanting to die. Who do you think they'll believe, you or me?"

I was afraid in the car with George, but foremost in my mind was how I would explain all this to Joel once I got home. He was a strong, self-confident police detective. How could he possibly identify with a timid, beaten down, petite woman afraid to stand up for herself? And how could I explain a stress and anxiety that I couldn't understand myself?

In the past I had always felt alone, and that the abuse was a shameful secret. The doctor had assured me that I was not alone anymore. "You have an official record of his abuse now," he told me, "and someone who loves and supports you. You're going to get through this." At one of the lowest points in my life (mostly because I felt I had embarrassed Joel) the doctor insisted I had a strength I didn't realize I possessed. "*You have sought out someone completely the opposite of your husband because you want a good life.*" His words rang in my memory and I hoped Joel's love was strong enough to weather this incident.

When Joel came home from work I was sitting on the bed, anxious. I tried to read his face as he walked in. He pulled me down on the bed beside him and held me for a moment, then pulled away and looked at me. I couldn't blame him for what he asked next. "Do you like being abused? Is that what you want, for me to abuse you?" I cried and said no. He hugged me again. And he didn't leave me. And we moved on from there. I was determined to do whatever I had to do so that I could have a life with this wonderful man who had done so much for me.

Gift From Within

I spent my lunch hour on my computer the next day, desperately searching for answers. I was on a mission. Typing my symptoms into the search engine was my first step: nightmares, intrusive disturbing thoughts, flashbacks, hypervigilance, among others. When Post Traumatic Stress Disorder came up I wasn't sure what it was. I kept reading and soon had a eureka moment. I wasn't crazy and my problem was certainly not unique. There was a name for what ailed me. Soon I found a website called "Gift from Within" (www.giftfromwithin.org). I spoke with the director who conducted a phone interview and invited me to join. The website was replete with helpful information. I learned about Complex PTSD which occurs with trauma that takes place repeatedly or over a period of time. It is common with childhood trauma and domestic abuse. The director encouraged me to find a trauma therapist.

Renee was a very patient and loving lady in her sixties who exuded patience, compassion and love. Herself a child victim of trauma, I had finally found a therapist who understood the fear I couldn't name. She knew there was more to leaving than simply moving out. My heart wanted to be free, but my mind had to also be free from the toxic shame of my past. I learned that it's okay to want to be strong and do it on my own, but it's also okay to need support. The most valuable gift she gave me was the permission to be on my side and the encouragement to be gentle with myself. "When you are injured, you pamper your injury until it heals. Your mind and emotions have been injured so pamper them" (my paraphrase). After I shared my story she surprised me by commenting that she was amazed I had survived this long, telling me I was stronger than I knew. I began to accept that my past was more detrimental than I had thought and that I was doing pretty well to have earned two degrees, managed a full time job for years, and functioned successfully each day.

I had consulted pastors, school counselors and psychologists in an effort to leave, over almost the entire twenty plus year span of my marriage. None of them ever thought to examine the emotional traumatic link between my past and my marriage to George.

Most women are told to make a plan, save money, have a safe place, etc. Those many women who keep going back are looked upon with disdain. They are called weak or stupid. No woman wants to be abused. If a woman feels emotionally trapped, there is probably something deeper going on.

I had opened a floodgate and I started devouring any material I could find about traumatic bonding and Stockholm Syndrome and how trauma can affect a victim of domestic violence. I had so far to go to be a happy, carefree person who could truly enjoy life. I felt very fortunate and blessed to have Joel in my life because he could read my moods so well and knew that he had a part in every victory I achieved.

In 2001 Joel helped his wife and girls move to central Florida to a farm that had plenty of land for their horses. Once they were settled, he went to visit them every weekend. I was proud of him for letting them know he was still going to be a part of their lives.

Chapter 9

Charlie

<u>2002</u>

*I*n 2002 we moved in to Joel's prior home, now vacated by the renters. My birthday was approaching so Joel took me to a ranch and led me into the back yard. There were beagles every-where! A man came up and led me to a huge pen where there was a beagle mom with a new batch of pups.

"Pick one out," Joel said to me.

Then the ranch owner reached in, grabbed a pup and placed him in my hands. I cuddled the beagle boy to my chest, and I couldn't give him back.

"This is the one," I said. "This is Charlie."

He tied a red string around Charlie's neck so no one else could choose him. I wouldn't be able to take him home until he was weaned, but I could visit him, and I did constantly. Now I had something little that needed me and depended on me. I was a mom! I always say Charlie is the best birthday present I ever received.

Eventually Joel sold the house and we moved in to a 40 foot RV. We would live in it for three years until we could retire. Joel still traveled to see his girls, now every two weeks. It was a blessing having Charlie with me while he was gone.

Visiting Charlie while his mom looks on from the pen;
Joel holding Charlie on one of our visits.

My buddy, always by my side; Charlie loved sitting
on the dash of the RV.

I remained close to George's mom, at times spending the night at her house while Joel was visiting his daughters, if it was safe for me to do so. She rarely cooked because cooking fumes bothered George. Any time she prepared food George would rush into the kitchen, throw the window open and turn on fans. She was mainly consisting on canned soup and TV dinners, and pizza delivered to the house. She had a toaster in her bathroom where she would toast bread in the mornings, or else she would microwave oatmeal. When I visited I would cook and then she would sometimes accompany me to the park, holding Charlie while I ran on the track.

A couple of times I had to leave her house hurriedly if George showed up. The last time I ever stayed he had held me against the wall, not letting me leave, until I yelled and his mom came out of her room. I never went back. Instead I would have his mom sneak out and meet me in a secret location where I would pick her up and take her to the RV and cook dinner for us. She spent my last Thanksgiving in Fort Lauderdale with me, and then I sent food home with her, admonishing her to tell George she had eaten at a friend's house.

November, 2007, Central Florida

On one of his trips to central Florida Joel got his divorce and, in 2006, I got mine. I visited three attorneys before finding one I felt safe with. A good friend loaned me the thousand dollars to pay the attorney. Before we left Fort Lauderdale, Joel and I went to the mall and picked out wedding bands.

In November of 2007 we moved in to my first house. Joel had it built on some land he owned in central Florida, not far from his girls. Joel had asked me, shortly after we met, to make a wish list of ten things. The first item was *a home of my own that no one can make me leave.* I had spent my whole life moving from place to place, with no permanency. And with George we had always lived in apartments until we moved in with his mom.

163

When we made our final move and I walked into our completed house, I went from room to room, crying. This time my tears were tears of joy.

"Thank you," I said to Joel. "It's so beautiful."

My Fairytale Wedding

On February 23, 2008 I walked down the aisle for the second time, this time in a small wedding chapel rather than a church. I had chosen white gold bands rather than yellow gold. We had written our own vows, rather than using the traditional ones. I wanted everything to be different this time. I had chosen "You Light Up My Life" by Debbie Boone rather than the Wedding March. Joel waited at the altar with his eyes pouring tears of happiness. As I walked towards him the words of that song declared how precious he was to me. When I saw his tears I knew I was really wanted this time.

The first time I married I somehow knew it wasn't right, that I wasn't loved or wanted the way a woman dreams of being wanted. What a difference this time! Joel and I had been together nearly eleven years and he still wanted me. Each one of his tears was a treasure, bottled up in my memory.

My strong handsome man waits for me; At 53, life has just begun.

Conclusion:

You Are Always Who You Were

<u>Present Day</u>

Our lives have settled into a comfortable routine. Every night we take Charlie on a golf cart ride, Charlie's favorite thing. Neighbors call the golf cart the Beaglemobile. Charlie considers the golf cart his personal "ride" and barks furiously if he sees his daddy on it without him. If other dogs approach the golf cart Charlie is not happy and tries to bark them away.

Charlie's "ride"

I still struggle with symptoms of my past. Nightmares occur in batches, sometimes on anniversaries of traumas I don't consciously remember. I've heard it said that it takes as long to heal as the trauma lasted. I don't know about that. I only know how thankful I am to have Joel by my side. He has an uncanny sense of when I'm hurting, and reacts with patience, kindness and support. I feel stronger every day I am with him. Each morning, when I awaken in his arms, I think, "God smiled on me." Every night when I cuddle up to him, I remind him, "This is my favorite place." He usually chuckles and reminds me of how I panicked when I heard he was coming to my squad.

I suffer at times from insecurity and trust issues. Joel doesn't get offended by that, but makes it his mission to prove to me that he is the man I think he is. He takes delight in doing things around the house that he knows make me happy. And I take delight in watching him work and observing how handy he is. It seems there is nothing he can't do. Some women get tired of having their husbands around underfoot and feel smothered, but I feel rather lost any time Joel goes somewhere without me. I love having him around and he says he feels the same about me.

One day I was functioning under the spell of a particularly bad nightmare. On our golf cart ride Joel pulled me close and leaned his head over on mine. Feeling comforted, I marveled at his uncanny ability to read me, and marveled at how comforting his touch always was. I began to compose a poem in my mind and quickly transferred it to paper when we got home. I left it on his desk that night before I went to bed:

168

My Favorite Place

Tonight you pulled me close to you as we rode on the cart.

I felt a love and strength that flowed to me straight from your heart.

The world around me dimmed away as you squeezed me so tight,

and I no longer felt the cold and dampness of the night.

I thought, "Whatever happens in the world can't touch me here,"

and marveled as the hurt I felt just seemed to disappear.

I felt this for the first time on that night so long ago,

with your first hug, when I had wished you'd never let me go.

It feels as good today and even better, if it can.

I rest within the strong arms of a giant of a man.

July 11, 2011

On the Beaglemobile

Why Couldn't I Leave?

A year is made up of 8,760 hours, 525,600 minutes and 31,536,000 seconds, and I endured each one of them while with George. I was trapped in a holding pattern, waiting to escape so my life could begin. I often felt like I was on a roller coaster, trapped in its ups and downs, having no control over where it took me, and being unable to get off. Living in a cyclical pattern of rewards and punishments, I was rewarded with calm if I did nothing wrong, sometimes even thrown a crumb of praise or a touch. I worked hard for those rewards and they kept me going. Committing one little infraction brought swift punishment in the form of hostility, silence, withholding of emotion, touch and speech, or angry tirades that left me trembling, tearful and terrified.

Most women are, by nature, caretakers. Because of my being forced into the role of saving my father's life, and the intense pity I felt for him when I should have simply been living out my childhood, my developing brain got stuck in that pattern. And so I also found myself pitying George, the second most important man in my life. My pity couldn't save him and he wasn't willing to work to save himself. I needed to save myself, but had been programmed to feel guilty for thinking about myself.

Constant criticism had me *feeling* I was less than smart. Toxic shame had me *convinced* I was bad. I *felt* unattractive, and unworthy of love. I *believed* leaving my marriage would offend God. Having no real emotional support I *felt* alone. All of these *feelings* were at play in my mind, and feelings *do* matter, but I didn't understand that. We're all responsible for our decisions and our actions. Or are we? We make decisions with the wisdom we've garnered through the years, and handle problems the way we've seen our caretakers handle theirs.

When many traumas occur, one on top of another, over a number of years, even the most resilient child can be buried under emotions and fears too extreme to handle, especially if no support system exists. As an adult, all of the fears I had as a little girl came back.

All of the things little Anna feared would happen if daddy died, I *felt* when George threatened to kill himself, or I *feared* would happen if I left him. I had to act against ingrained feelings, beliefs and fears that were enmeshed in me. And, again, feelings *do* matter!

It went beyond pity for dad and George. A child depends on her parents for life. If a parent dies or goes away, the child feels she may die as well. The whole foundation of my life was shaky from my mom's neglect, when I was a toddler; my father's suicide attempts, as a young child; and then by the lack of stability as I was handed off from relative to relative and moved from town to town and school to school. By the time I married George I was in no way strong enough, wise enough or prepared by life to handle an abusive husband. Dysfunction had been my life-long norm.

One day, during my struggle to escape George, it dawned on me that if it was frightening living with him, and leaving was frightening, I might as well leave because either way I would have to endure a period of pain. I had to decide which pain was worse and which out-come was best. At least, if I left, the pain wouldn't go on forever. If I stayed, the pain would last the rest of my life. My tender hearted nature pitied George, but I would never be able to rescue him. It was, to use George's own words, "an exercise in futility." I decided to save myself. But, as I strove to leave, my biggest revelation was: *I had to look back before I could move forward because we are always who we were.*

Meeting Joel awakened me to a whole new existence. Under the comfort and safety of his amazing love I began to blossom, grow and heal. With George I had lost myself. Joel gave so much back to me that I had lost, including myself. And that was the best gift of all.

171

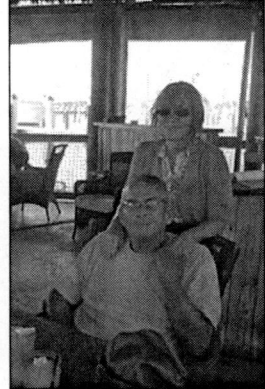

St. Augustine, 2013

I lost all my family of origin and never started a family with George, but, with Joel and Charlie, I now have my own little family of three. Thanks to my step-daughters I also have three wonderful grandchildren who bring lots of joy and smiles. Someday they may question why they have three grandmothers but, for now, I'm just enjoying being "gammy".

Holding the first precious one to call me Gammy,
at my surprise 60th birthday party.

~~~~~~~~~~~~~~~

I finished this draft to present to Joel on our sixth wedding anniversary. I signed the publishing contract, unintentionally, on what would have been the 36th anniversary of my marriage to George. Coincidence? I don't think so.

Endnotes

[1] "In My Own Little Corner," from Rodgers and Hammerstein's *Cinderella*, 1963.

[2] Oliver, Mary. <u>New and Selected Poems Volume One</u>. Boston, Massachusetts: Beacon Press. 1992. Page 114.

<u>Suggested Helpful Resources</u>

<u>Online Support</u>

<u>www.giftfromwithin.org</u> An online support group for women with post traumatic stress disorder.

<u>www.goodtherapy.org</u> Resource for help in locating a therapist.

www.sidran.org "We help people understand, manage, and treat trauma and dissociation.

www.ncvc.org The National Center for Victims of Crime.

www.ncadv.org The National Coalition Against Domestic Violence.

www.abanet.org/domviol American Bar Association Commission on Domestic Violence.

www.trynova.org For victims of crime.

Hotlines

National Domestic Violence Hotline: 1-800-799-7233 (SAFE)

National Suicide Prevention Hotline: 1-800-273-8255 (TALK)

Books

(PTSD and Complex PTSD)

Complex PTSD: From Surviving to Thriving by Pete Walker.

Trauma and Recovery by Judith Herman.

No Comfort Zone: Notes on Living with Post Traumatic Stress Disorder by Marla Handy. Note: Interview with Marla Handy available through Gift From Within http://www.giftfromwithin.org

Trust After Trauma by Aphrodite Matsakis, Ph.D.

Before the World Intruded by Michele Rosenthal.

<u>Waking the Tiger: Healing Trauma</u> by Peter A. Levine.

<u>The Body Bears the Burden: Trauma, Dissociation, and Disease</u> by Robert C. Scaer, M.D.

<u>The Body Remembers: The Psychophysiology of Trauma and Trauma Treatment</u> by Babette Rothschild.

<u>(Domestic Abuse)</u>

<u>Pastor's Handbook on Domestic Violence</u> by Voliea Olmoguez. Available through Zoe University (904-725-0400).

<u>The Verbally Abusive Relationship</u> by Patricia Evans. Also <u>Controlling People; Verbal Abuse Survivors Speak Out;</u> and <u>Victory Over Verbal Abuse</u> by the same author.

<u>The Emotionally Abusive Relationship</u> by Beverly Engel.

<u>Traumatic Bonding And The Development Of The Stockholm Syndrome in Battered Women</u> by Debra Dixon.

<u>No Visible Wounds: Identifying Nonphysical Abuse of Women by Their Men</u> by Mary Susan Miller, Ph.D.

(Abandonment and Loneliness)

The God Who is There and He is There and He is not Silent by Francis Schaeffer, Swiss Philosopher and Theologian.

The Furious Longing of God and Abba's Child by Brennan Manning.

Man's Search for Meaning by Viktor Frankl, survivor of Auschwitz Concentration Camp.

Black Swan and The Journey from Abandonment to Healing by Susan Anderson.

Children of the Self-Absorbed by Nina W. Brown.

The Emotionally Absent Mother by Jasmin Lee Cori.

(Self-Harming)

Freedom from Self-Harm by Kim L. Gratz and Alexander L. Chapman.

Women Who Hurt Themselvs: A Book of Hope and Understanding by Dusty Miller.

(Healthy Relationships)

For Men Only and For Women Only by Shaunti and Jeff Feldhahn.

Beyond the Marriage Fantasy by Daniel Beaver.

<u>Strike the Original Match</u> by Dr. Charles R. Swindoll.

<u>The Seven Principles of Making Marriage Work</u> by John Gottman.

Articles

"Constructive Desertion as A Ground for Divorce: 'Jane Eyre' circa 2006" available from NAMI (National Alliance for the Mentally Ill) <u>http://md.nami.org</u>

"Understanding the Victims of Spousal Abuse" by Frank M. Ochberg, M.D. <u>http://www.giftfromwithin.org</u>

"Complex PTSD" by Julia M. Whealin, Ph.D. <u>http://www.ncptsd.org</u>

"Scars that Won't Heal: The Neurobiology of Child Abuse" by Martin H. Teicher. <u>http://www.annafoundation.org/stwh.html</u>

"Abusive Relationships: Trauma Bonding" by Julia Crane. http://www.counsellingwestonsupermare.co.uk/featured/trauma-bonding

"Why Don't They Just Leave? The Theory of Learned Helplessness" www.ojp.usdoj.gov/ovc/assis/

"Trauma Bonding" by Michael Samsel http://www.abuseandrelationships.org

Article about Cptsd, <u>http://www.svfreenyc.org/survivors_factsheet_97.html</u>

Article about Stockholm syndrome in battered women, http://forum. psychlinks.ca/abuse-domestic-violence-child-abuse/3069-battered-women-traumatic-bonding-and-the-stockholm-syndrome.html

---

* For more reading suggestions, visit the Book Review page at http:// www.giftfromwithin.org and take advantage of the videos and podcasts too.

CPSIA information can be obtained at www.ICGtesting.com
Printed in the USA
LVOW11s0254110915

453714LV00001B/109/P